Sto

FINDING GOD'S HEALING POWER

But without faith it is impossible to please Him: for he that cometh to God must believe that He is, and that He is a rewarder of them that diligently seek Him.

—HEBREWS 11:6

Finding

God's

Healing Power

By Gertrude D. McKelvey

J. B. LIPPINCOTT COMPANY

PHILADELPHIA AND NEW YORK

First Edition

Printed in the United States of America

Library of Congress Catalog Card Number: 61-8156

1143355

To John

AUTHOR'S NOTE

The names of those who have given of their time and experience that this book might be written would make a long list indeed. However, without the help of these many persons I could never have attempted to deal with a subject so infinitely mysterious, nor could I hope to have conveyed a deeper understanding of how God's gift of healing love may be gained through the churches. To all these unnamed I am greatly indebted.

CONTENTS

IV HEALING THROUGH THE CHURCH
    CLINIC

V HEALING THROUGH PASTORAL
    COUNSELING

VI THINK ON THESE THINGS

INTRODUCTION

This book is intended to take you on an exciting adventure: an adventure at times mysterious and incomprehensible, yet understandable and simple. A mystery when applied to your life will give it depth, breadth, and glorious meaning. Never again will your life be dull. Never again will you entertain for long the devastating emotion of boredom.

For nine years I have been seeking out people, most of them unknown, a few famous, both rich and poor. Some have had educational advantages and some little or none. But all of them possess one essential ingredient: love's healing power. These persons learned through suffering and heartache how to find and use the healing powers within themselves— the gift of God—which He created within their minds, souls and bodies.

We are all possessors of these divine gifts, yet too few of us use them as God intended. There are many reasons why. You will learn them from the healing experiences of those you will meet in the pages of this book.

The healing of the body by faith through prayer is greatly misunderstood by the average sick person and by many members of the Christian church.

As I look back upon thirty years as a minister's wife, I know that many times I have been brought face to face with God's miraculous power when it was released in the lives of those I served. However, it took a long time for me to awaken to the fact that God's *healing power* is something He wishes us to use every day, even every minute of our lives.

Like many good church members I looked upon faith-healing with caution. I have never doubted that God could do anything. No miracle was too big for my God to perform, but I did not like the methods some of our present-day "healers" were using. It was Dr. E. Stanley Jones, internationally known missionary, himself an example of God's healing power, who said, "The queer have queered it for us." I am afraid I believed that people could be healed by God's power if it were done in a quiet, so-called "respectable" way.

I hasten to add that I still do not like the mass psychology that is practiced under big canvas tents, or in rented theaters and stadiums, but I have long ago ceased to be critical of those who serve God in ways which to me sometimes are downright shocking! I have learned, moreover, that God uses all of us in spite of ourselves, and He asks us to leave the judging of others exclusively to Him.

It was in this frame of mind that I accepted an assignment from Dr. T. Otto Nall, then editor-in-chief of the former *Christian Advocate*, to attend a healing service at St. Stephen's Episcopal Church in Philadelphia. If I found a story there, I was to do a feature on it for him. My experience that day is related in Part II of this book. Suffice it to say here that from that day on I began to study divine healing in earnest.

After visiting St. Stephen's I turned to my Bible and began reading it in the light of healing by faith. I discovered that the spiritual healing of the body, mind, and soul, with or without the aid of medicine, *is not a new discovery*. It is the age-old story of God's loving power at work in the lives of His children, who turn to Him *believing* that He alone gives healing. I was assured that God *does heal*, that through His Son many were healed and in many different ways. Not once did anyone come to Jesus, sincerely and faithfully, and go away without receiving a blessing of some kind. He healed some who had no faith; some who had great faith He did *not* heal, among them Paul, who carried his "thorn in the flesh" all the years he faithfully served his Lord.

The book of Acts describes the beginning of the Christian church and reveals the place of Christ's healing power in establishing Christianity. In fact it was this miraculous healing of the sick that attracted many followers. Ancient history reveals a shocking state of affairs regarding those who sought good health. Doctors, and these far from good, were at a premium; they were expensive and located only in the largest metropolitan areas. Many poor, desperate souls, in their struggle for health, believed they could not even turn to their god or gods. The gods preferred healthy worshipers. If one had financial means and could not find a doctor, he might journey to the temple and pay an exorbitant fee to the priest, who would intercede in his behalf with his god.

But with Christ's death upon the Cross, salvation both of body and soul became available in the world. Jesus' compassion filled the hearts of His apostles and His many followers. The poor, the desperate, the lost found in Christianity an oasis for their broken bodies and sick minds. Acts 2:43 says "And many wonders and signs were done by the apostles." And Luke tells us "And the seventy returned again with joy, saying, Lord, even the devils are subject unto us through thy name" (10:17).

Yet, as the organized church came into being, and emperors professed Christianity as they took power because it was expedient to do so, the memory of Pentecost gradually grew dim. The church became corrupted with political power as Christians turned from Christ, filled with obsessions of their own importance. When the Roman Emperor Constantine made Christianity the state religion, it was not only stylish to be a Christian but downright healthy political strategy as well.

Dr. Leslie Weatherhead says in his *Psychology, Religion and Healing*, "It was a disaster that Constantine was converted. He may have seen a cross in the sky, but he produced a Christianity that left out the cross, and might as well have made a cushion its symbol. Christianity became, in fact, a polite veneer without power or beauty."

When the source from which the vital healing power came was ignored, a decline in healing results was inevitable. Then as always, when Christian discipline relaxes, the church weakens.

Although the church became corrupt and the Cross merely a pretty symbol, worn indiscreetly by most, there remained the faithful few; because of them, praying for the sick was continued by Christians down through the ages. The early church fathers from St. Justin Martyr (100-165) to St. Jerome (340-420) still reported some healings through anointing with oil (often that from the lamps of the church, which was blessed), through the laying-on-of-hands and the use of holy water. All these methods, of course, were supported by prayers for the sick.

Individuals still believing in the power of prayer continued to pray for the healing of the sick, from St. Bernard of Clairvaux (1091-1153) and St. Francis of Assisi to Martin Luther and the Reformation, and from Luther down to the beginnings of the larger denominations of the Protestant church with such men as John Wesley, the founder of Methodism.

And the Christian church today, in this twentieth century of atomic power and guided missiles, is experiencing a resurgence of God's healing power with which it was born.

Today leaders in religion, science, and medicine are saying of this resurgence in the church: "It is about time!" Dr. Paul E. Johnson, head of the Department of Psychology of Religion at Boston University, says: "The church has an inescapable responsibility for the spiritual health of mankind." And Carl Steinmetz, the electrical wizard, once said: "The greatest discoveries of the twentieth century will come in the realm of the spirit."

The two great sources of healing, medicine and religion, are not only working side by side in many new and interesting ways but are studying the whole man—body, mind and soul—in an effort to meet the desperate human needs of our day. There are signs that we of this century are turning to a new obedience to God's will, over and above the great discoveries of our atomic age, to a deeper trust in God's mercy and in the salvation of *His power.* There is also a great deal of evidence that physical healings are being realized within the realm of the church, *often after all hope of medical cure is gone.*

The Christian church slowly but surely is rising to face this hour which, I have no doubt, will be her most shining one. Because of the many reports of spiritual healing continually coming from the Protestant churches, in 1950 the National Council of Churches conducted a survey under its commission on Religion and Health. Dr. Charles S. Braden, Professor of History and Literature of Religions at Northwestern University, who headed the survey, gives a clear picture of its aims when he states: "My own experience with the minority groups, which almost all engage in spiritual healing, has led me to wonder whether the practice was limited to them or *was being carried on in the larger denominations.*"

Nine hundred and eighty-two letters were sent to twenty-seven key people, located both in large cities and rural areas across our country. These key persons distributed the questionnaires to ministers within their area. The first question, which asked, "Have you ever as a minister attempted to perform a spiritual healing?," clearly stated the information sought. The two-page questionnaire then proceeded on a how, when, where, basis. Dr. Braden states, "In the course of the study a great many cases were described in considerable detail."

The following case points up, I feel, the earnestness with which the minister of a large Midwestern Methodist church willingly became a channel through which God's wisdom and power could flow.

This minister received an urgent call to the hospital bed of the wife of one of his parishioners. Meeting the surgeon in the corridor, he asked, "Is it so serious, Doctor?" "Yes," replied the doctor; "a matter of hours." Entering the patient's room, the minister found her conscious and able to talk.

"Quite sick, aren't you?" he asked.

"Yes, very sick," answered the patient.

"One of the interesting experiences in my life as a minister is in watching folks come into the hospital so very sick, even as you are, and then go out in a short time in good health."

"That is wonderful," she said.

"Well, that is for you, too," said the minister.

"Oh, I wish it were."

"Tell me," he went on, "how old is your little daughter?"

"Ten years old."

"Just the age when she needs you most, don't you agree?"

"Yes, she does," answered the mother.

"All right," said the minister, "remember you have a great and powerful God, and remember the doctors and nurses are doing everything to help you. Now we are going to have communion, but I want you to promise me that you will make a hard fight to stay around for your husband and your daughter. You will do that, won't you?"

She promised and she was there the next day, when the minister called again. Gradually she made a complete recovery. Her surgeon, meeting the minister later, remarked, "Well, I didn't do it. God did. According to my time schedule she would be in Heaven now, but instead she is at home in good health."

Dr. Braden reports:

On tabulating the various diseases I found I had listed sixty-four which were different enough to note separately. On closer examination many of these fell into broad, general classes. I was interested to note that the largest number of these were of cancer of one kind or another: cancer of lung, mouth, spine, duodenal, bone, etc. Did the patient really have cancer? In almost every case the informant declared that the diagnosis had been made by a competent doctor and that there had been medical attendance for a longer or shorter period. One case of lung cancer that had persisted for two years had been properly diagnosed and treated by a physician. After the healing (which consisted of the laying-on-of-hands, some ritual and prayer at a healing service) X-ray tests disclosed that the condition had cleared and in a period of six months, prior to the time of reporting the case, there had been no recurrence.

I highly recommend this fine report, which I believe is the first of its kind in the United States. As Dr. Braden so aptly puts it, "It is at the very least a report of what ministers firmly believe has happened as a result of their ministry of healing."

I, too, wondered what our larger denominations were doing in the churches through spiritual healing. I must admit that having once begun to study this subject I could not stop. And out of my study has grown this book—the story of the ways in which the larger denominations of the Protestant church are bringing healing to many physically ill and emotionally disturbed people.

It is not a survey but rather a panoramic view of the spiritual healing that is taking place in our churches today. Healing takes place in many and varied ways, as you will learn from those who share their healing experiences with you in the pages of this book. Some few have been healed in an instant, miraculously, without the aid of science. Some have received healing over a longer period with the aid of medicine and spiritual therapy, still others with the help of a church clinic or a church-related psychiatrist.

You will meet patients whom surgeons and physicians call "miracle cases" and learn of the ever-growing teamwork between physicians and clergymen who believe that all healing is a gift from God. You will be inspired with the reactions of young men in theological training who lay aside their pulpit gowns to put on the stiff white coats of hospital orderlies that they may better understand the mind and soul of a suffering body.

Last but not least, you will learn how you can discover and use God's healing power in your own life. You can have good health. You can help others to have it. You can have the abundant life our Lord lived, died, and rose again to make available for you and for me.

I

* * *

Healing Through

Your Doctor

1 * DOCTOR, PATIENT
AND SPIRITUAL HEALING

Wesley Hablett* opened his eyes to see his surgeon standing quietly by his bed. He realized slowly that the doctor, whom we shall call Dr. Jones, had come to give him the final report on his operation. His thoughts now went back to his conversation with the surgeon just before entering the hospital.

"Dr. Jones, I can take it. I'm a grown man," he had said. "So promise me you will tell me the truth when you know it."

Five full days had passed since he had been wheeled back to his bed from surgery. For the other patients about him in the small ward this period meant healing and recovery.

About his own case he was not so sure, since his operation had been performed to remove a malignant tumor from his spine. Now he would learn the truth.

Dr. Jones was reviewing the operation. He had found it possible to remove only part of the tumor, since cancer had spread, making it difficult to determine where the diseased cells stopped and the healthy cells began.

Fifty-year-old Wesley Hablett, sensing the truth, went right to the point. "How long have I got, Dr. Jones?" he asked.

* The names of those whose stories appear in this book are fictitious except in certain cases—as that of Wesley Hablett—where the author has been given permission to use real names.

This outstanding neurological surgeon, a man of great faith, pulled the curtain around his patient's bed to insure privacy and sat down. This was not the first time he had been compelled to bring a hopeless report, yet each time it seemed more difficult.

He gave the answer quickly. "If you want to know how long I *think* you will live, then I would say about six months. But we both know that only God knows the answer."

A long silence followed, one of those times when, as so often happens in a doctor-patient relationship, a feeling of trust, compassion and gratitude akin to love possessed each. The surgeon broke the silence by asking: "Would you like me to pray with you?"

Wesley Hablett nodded. The surgeon's hand slipped into his pocket, came up with a small Testament from which he read quietly, then prayed. Another silence followed as these two men thought of their Saviour and His redeeming love. They had not asked for healing but for strength to carry out God's will for their lives.

Two weeks later Dr. Jones was able to discharge his patient, who had begun to recover as normally as the other patients in the beds about him. At home, after four months of convalescence, Wesley Hablett went back to work at his old job as stockman for the Reading Railroad. Since then, he has not lost a day's work because of illness. Every June and December he makes an important trip to Philadelphia to a medical center to undergo clinical tests, just to make sure the cancer has not returned. This center has a full record on Mr. Hablett's case from the time he entered the hospital for his operation up to the present. He has remained in excellent physical condition for the past seven years, and his clinical tests, since the first six months after his operation, have all been negative.

My first interview with Dr. Jones confirmed my convictions that doctors who practice their religion with their surgery and medicine can better serve their patients. They are not always surprised when they witness a so-called "miracle" case, for they know the ideals of the medical profession are identical with those of the Christian ministry.

Dr. Jones makes clear his belief that God's power is unlimited if in His wisdom God ordains that that power be used for the spiritual healing of the physical body.

"I believe that all healing is from God," he told me.

"Do you make it a regular habit to pray with your patients?" I asked.

"No, only when I feel the occasion demands it. But I often feel I should take the time to do so more frequently, not only for the patient but because it is good for me too, you know."

"Have you seen Mr. Hablett recently?" I asked.

"Not recently," answered Dr. Jones. "I did see him several times after I discharged him from the hospital. Later I turned him back to his local doctor. We have exchanged several letters during the past five years."

"What were your thoughts and feelings the morning you told Mr. Hablett of his condition?"

"My heart went out to him not only because of what I knew or thought I knew was ahead of him, but because he had such a grand spirit about it all," Dr. Jones said. "However, I did feel I should obey the desire to pray and that, I knew, would strengthen both of us."

"Did you feel an uplifting of the spirit at that time?" I asked.

"Yes," he answered in a quiet tone. "We had a wonderful time together as we read the New Testament and prayed."

It is interesting to note that when I put the same question to Wesley Hablett he was to answer with the same words: "We had a wonderful time together."

It was some time after my interview with Dr. Jones that I met Wesley Hablett and his wife, Louise, for the first time.

"What did you think about, lying there in your hospital

bed after Dr. Jones had gone and you knew your days were numbered?" was the first question I put to him. He is a stockily built man of average height, who fairly glows with good health.

"Many thoughts came crowding into my mind," he said, "as I reviewed my life. I realized there was so much I had not done that I hoped I could yet do, but one thought came repeatedly: If I am to be healed now, only God can do it. I believed He could if it was His will. Dr. Jones's prayer had given me a great peace. I did not even feel concerned, for I knew my life was in God's hands now."

Wesley Hablett told me that he was not only healed physically but that he was changed spiritually as well. "I used to go to church occasionally, just to please Louise, but now I go because I want to go," he said. "It's a real joy to be in church and to work for God's kingdom through it."

Louise Hablett told me about some of the work her husband does at the Port Carbon Methodist Church, where they are members, serving in an official capacity as well as in other ways.

Wesley Hablett gives God full credit for his miraculous healing and he feels that God used his surgeon, for whom he carries a deep affection, in bringing about his complete and miraculous recovery.

Recently he wrote me, "My wife and I are in the best of health and enjoying every minute of it. Today and yesterday we had a real blizzard and the old back was given a good workout shoveling snow, but didn't mind it a bit."

I learned that Dr. Jones is a member of the Christian Medical Society, an outstanding organization to maintain inspiration for Christian service among physicians and medical students. Its main purpose is to witness to the redeeming power of Christ.

Dr. Jones and his patient would heartily agree with the convictions of Dr. Richard C. Cabot, a renowned physician at the Massachusetts General Hospital, who was a pioneer in convincing doctors that more than medicine is required in restoring health. He looked upon medicine and religion as powerful allies.

And Dr. Andrew D. Elia, Assistant Professor of Obstetrics and Gynecology at Boston University, gave this challenge to his students: "Above all, the physicians themselves must realize that they have a great mission to perform. They are ministers of the soul as well as healers of pain and regulators of disturbed physiology and anatomy. Theirs is a high calling. Their work is never routine and their relationship with the patient is akin to the holy."

2 * HEALING'S TRIUMPHANT MYSTERY

Dr. Bernard Hollander, in his extensive study entitled *In Search of the Soul*, writes: "Instead of saying that man has a soul, it would be more correct to say that man himself is a soul. He is not a conscious machine but a spiritual being."

Some of the greatest physicians of our day believe that the pendulum is swinging from the concept of man as largely physical to that of man as formed in the image of God and therefore infinitely spiritual. In his book, *Psychology, Religion, and Human Need*, Dr. W. L. Carrington says:

> The surgeon may perform a brilliant operation for the removal of a gangrenous appendix, or some other organ or tissue which may be interfering with a person's health, but the surgeon's knife has no healing power. The healing power of God in the patient has to heal the operation area and the surgeon's wound and restore the patient's health.

The physician, by using penicillin or some other antibiotic, may upset the reproductive power of the germs and in so doing, bring about the recovery of many people from disease, which would otherwise have been fatal or highly dangerous. But penicillin has no power to heal any of the inflamed and poisoned tissues, nor can it clean up the mess left by the action of the germs. The healing power of God in the patient has to do that.

If we stop to think about it, we will realize that at this very moment we who are well are rightly so because our body is at work through our blood and cells fighting off the germs we are constantly taking into the body in one way or another. The wonderful functioning of the body keeps us well. And who made our marvelous bodies? We could conjecture end-lessly about the laws of nature and the mystery of death and how it leaves the body an empty shell. But the spirit of the body lives on. This is the Christian's belief. Romans 8 tells us that we are more than flesh. Paul wrote: "But if the spirit of Him that raised up Jesus from the dead dwell in you, He that raised up Christ from the dead shall also quicken your mortal bodies by His Spirit that dwelleth in you" (Romans 8:11).

But we are concerned here about the working power of the spirit of God within us, day by day. This is the gift of life while we are still on the earth. We must believe that God is within us, right now. "For in Him we live, and move, and have our being; as certain also of your own poets have said, For we are also His offspring." This is the way Paul explained it to the Athenians on Mars Hill (Acts 17:28).

Dr. Claude Forkner, Professor of Chemical Medicine at Cornell University, agrees that healing is a mystery, for an article in the magazine *Clear Horizons* quotes him as say-ing: "Very often we do not know what it is that brings about recovery of a patient. I am sure that very often it is faith which is the important factor!"

We do not doubt that when Jesus said, "Be thou whole,"

He meant as a unit of body, mind and soul. And to Him the
soul was most important. Dr. Allan Hunter, the well-known
California clergyman, writes in *Clear Horizons*, in an article
entitled, "The New Teamwork Between Medicine and
Faith":

> There is a mystery—deep, deep, mystery—in the relationship of
> faith to medicine and no one need be under pressure to come
> up with all the answers. But we all need to be clear on one
> point: there is no enmity between the best technique of the
> doctor's office or the surgeon's operating table, and the best ex-
> pression of ungullible humble faith. Present-day medicine aims
> at removing the blocks to the immeasurable and amazing powers
> of recovery that God has put in our bodies.

Without exception all the persons whom I have interviewed for this book, and the ministers engaged in a spiritual
healing ministry through the organized church, firmly believe
that God often uses both medicine and spiritual therapy in
restoring health. There are also, as we have said, many re-
corded cases throughout history and in our own day of cures
that have taken place without the aid of a doctor or after all
medical efforts have failed. We are now opening our minds
to the fact that there are available to us greater aids to healing through the realm of the spirit than we have in the past
been willing to admit.

Dr. A. P. Waterson, M.D., M.R.C.P., Reach Fellow at
Emmanuel College, Cambridge, says in a recent number of
Christian Medical Fellowship: "It takes considerable humility
on the part of the doctor to realize how much in healing for
which he is given credit, is not really to his credit at all."

Only faith can bring peace and confidence to the patient
about to undergo an operation, especially for the first time.
This outlook is not only accepted but encouraged in the
patient's mind in many hospitals today. This is particularly
so in world-famous Bellevue, in New York City. In this great

city hospital eleven clergymen are members of the staff. These chaplains, some maintained by the city of New York, represent the Catholic, Jewish and Protestant faiths. Often representatives of various other creeds and beliefs are called in to meet the patients' spiritual needs.

The second floor of the administration building of Bellevue is appropriately called Chapel Hall, for it houses three good-sized sanctuaries called chapels. Chapel Hall also contains offices and consultation rooms for the chaplains of each of the three faiths.

As do many other hospitals today, Bellevue has a continuous program, in the form of a twelve-week series of lectures, for the clinical training of young clergymen. The classes, taught by the staff chaplains, deal with the use of religious psychology for the ill. Often staff doctors or supervising nurses are invited to lecture. In white coats with blue armbands labeled "Chaplain-Intern," these clergymen learn how to visit the sick, bringing to the patients comfort and assurance that God is with them through every ordeal. After visiting patients, they make notes on their conversations, which are discussed in class later. Any mistakes made by the young clergymen are noted, to be rectified in future visits.

It is a rule at Bellevue that every patient about to undergo an operation must talk with one of the chaplains. The chaplain can postpone an operation if he feels the patient is not emotionally ready to undergo surgery.

In the best-selling book, *Bellevue Is My Home,* Arthur and Barbara Gelb draw a fascinating picture of the hospital by tracing the activities of the Deputy Medical Superintendent, Dr. Salvatore R. Cutolo. The following excerpt from the chapter on "Prayer and Medicine" best illustrates a most important part of the chaplain's work.

A woman patient had undergone an exploratory operation the day before the chaplain's visit and was about to undergo another.

The woman, pale and trembling, moaned, "Oh, Chaplain, don't let them take me to the operating room again. I'm not strong enough. I just can't do it. Don't let anyone talk me into signing a release for another operation!"

The chaplain, aware that the operation must be a necessary and urgent one if the doctors had called for it so soon after the first one, refrained from stressing this logical, medical fact, which he felt sure must have already been pointed out to her. Instead he tried to respond to her emotional reaction on her own terms. "Do you go to church?" he asked. "Do you have a religious faith of any kind?" "Yes, I believe very strongly," she replied.

"Do you believe that God's power can come to people?"

"Yes, I believe that, too," she answered. "But I don't even have enough strength to ask for His power."

"But you have reached out to me for help and you and I together can reach out for God's strength."

"Do you really think we can?" asked the woman in a faint voice.

The chaplain assured her that she could and holding her hands in his, he prayed that God's strength and healing power pour into her. As the prayer drew to a close, the woman grew relaxed and limp. She leaned back against her pillows with a long sigh. "I can go up to the operating room now," she murmured.

At Bellevue and in many other hospitals throughout the world it has been proved repeatedly that the minister's visit with the patient during the pre-operative period can be of invaluable aid to the doctor and particularly to the anesthetist. A patient filled with apprehension can give the anesthetist a difficult time, as anxiety causes the body to release adrenalin, which results in an increased heart beat, rise in blood pressure, a muscular rigidity, and sometimes nausea and vomiting. All of these conditions tend to counteract the action of the premedication as well as that of the anesthetic drugs. Naturally this means complicated surgery for the doctor, a stormy induction of the drug for the patient, as well as difficult maintenance of the drug during the operation.

But how different an operation can be for a patient who is aware of God's abiding Presence, and is filled with love and confidence in those about him who are working for his welfare. The patient in this frame of mind has no apprehensions. His faith means that he needs less anesthesia; his body relaxes and he maintains a stable blood pressure. And on his hospital chart his doctor is able to write: Recovery uneventful.

3 * I ENJOYED MY OPERATION

A ridiculous title, isn't it? You are probably thinking, Is this silly woman about to tell about her operation? Yes, I am, but with a different slant. I wish to share with you my own experience of some years ago, as I was able to overcome all fear by putting the thought of trust in its place.

I can truthfully say I did enjoy three-quarters of my hospital experience, allowing one-quarter for the inevitable pain. I can also say it was one of the outstanding spiritual experiences of my life and I would not have missed it for anything.

The day my doctor told me surgery would be necessary I went home from his office in a half-daze, thinking what many others in the same situation have thought: Other people have operations but it just can't happen to me! I also dreaded the thought of spinal anesthesia, which he had recommended.

"Oh, Doctor," I protested. "Not for me. I don't want to be conscious and know what is going on."

He laughed. "You needn't be." He suggested I go home and think over the advantages. With a spinal I would have no nausea after the operation and my recovery would be more rapid.

For the next three days I lived through a struggle over the human side of me. I am not brave. The thought of pain is frightening to me and my vivid imagination under these circumstances was full of negative thoughts. At home for the next three days I worried through my duties in a semi-fog. Even my prayers did not bring the peace I needed.

I knew better than to worry in this way but I could not help it. I was crossing one imaginary bridge after another. I even remembered having read that the largest percentage of operations are performed on patients who are "walk-ins," meaning those who were not sick enough to be carried into the hospital. For these, anticipation can be and often is, downright mental torture. I was a "walk-in." How I longed to be too sick to care what happened.

The fourth morning I picked up my Bible and turned to the eighth chapter of Romans: "Who shall separate us from the love of Christ? Shall tribulation, or distress, or persecution, or famine, or nakedness, or peril, or sword? Nay, in all these things we are more than conquerors through Him that loved us. For I am persuaded, that neither death, nor life, nor angels, nor principalities, nor powers, nor things present, nor things to come, nor height, nor depth, nor any other creature, shall be able to separate us from the love of God, which is in Christ Jesus our Lord" (Romans 8:37-39).

At last reassuring peace took possession of my mind.

As it turned out I had to wait three months before having the operation, yet I felt no more apprehension of what lay ahead. I was busy and happy even through the periods of ill health brought on by my condition.

On entering the hospital, however, I suddenly had another battle to win. I underwent a mixed emotion of loneliness, a depression which comes, I suppose, with separation from one's family and entry into the strange new world of a hospital. Anticipating surgery, especially for the first time, one naturally feels the strain of what may lie ahead. My room had a bareness about it and the high bed I knew I would be living in for the major part of the next two weeks was far from inspiring. Then I was flabbergasted by the unexpected hospital brigade of nurses, interns and the anesthetist arriving at intervals to examine me. And their questioning about the history of my health from childhood to the present reminded me of a psychiatrist bent on depth analysis.

It was during this period of hospital orientation that I welcomed a visit from the Reverend George Lurwick, minister of St. Luke's Methodist Church, Bryn Mawr. I shall always be grateful to George, who is a personal friend, for treating me like any other patient. He knew that, even though I was a minister's wife, I was also a human being, in need of spiritual help at this particular time. I've mentioned that my husband is a minister, but our prayers together in the hospital were as husband and wife, much like those of any other couple, not as minister and parishioner.

My operation was scheduled for eight o'clock the following morning. I awoke at six after a good night's sleep, having taken the prescribed drug. I later learned that some anxiety-filled patients fail to sleep before an operation regardless of the amount of drugs administered. I had finally agreed with my doctor and the head anesthetist to have a spinal after they assured me I would be pleasantly drowsy.

I got out of bed, sat by the window, and reread the eighth chapter of Romans. The last trace of fear slipped from me as I watched the dawn break through a heavy January fog. Then I wrote in my diary: "I am completely at peace. God is very dear and close. His love enfolds me. I know I must walk in the dark for a short time, but it will help me better to understand those who suffer. Dear God, help me in this experience to be all You want me to be."

I climbed back into bed and in a few minutes the efficient routine began as nurses and interns prepared me for surgery. I could hardly believe I was about to have an operation. By the time my husband arrived, I had been given the pre-operative drug. Wrapped in a warm sheet and already on a stretcher I was about to be wheeled out of my room. I was so comfortable that I did not want to open my eyes. "Don't worry about me," I told John, as he kissed me. "I'm not afraid and I'm ready."

The drug had taken effect. I wanted to sleep and I dozed off. I do not remember being wheeled down the corridor into the elevator or being taken up to the operating area on the fifth floor. However, the anesthetist's voice saying "Good morning, Mrs. McKelvey" awakened me. "Are you ready?" he asked.

"Yes, what do you want me to do?"

"Oh, just curl up in a little ball." He laughed softly as the nurse and the doctor pulled me into the right position. I felt three little taps along my spine and it was over. I was on my back again being wheeled into the operating room. My doctor came in and patted my hand. His eyes smiled at me above his white mask. My feet began to feel warm; I have never felt more comfortable.

Suddenly I began to take an interest in everything going on about me. On the ceiling was a large mirror. When the anesthetist's nurse laid soft, cool pads on my eyes, I was annoyed at not being able to see, and asked my doctor if he would mind if I watched him.

"Go right ahead. Look up into the mirror and enjoy yourself," he said. The nurse removed the pads from my eyes.

I asked the nurse, who spoke to me now and then, if she would tell me when the doctor started to operate. Presently, I heard her say, "Mrs. McKelvey, Dr. Richards is beginning now."

I looked up into the mirror. I had a grand feeling of detachment; it was almost as if I were watching a movie flashed on the ceiling for my entertainment. I had a feeling of deep contentment which remained throughout the operation. How much of this feeling was produced by drugs and how much was in answer to my prayers I will never know. I am satisfied in believing that God did answer my prayers and kept His promise that "all things work together for good to them that trust Him."

The operation, an hour and a half in duration, seemed to pass in fifteen minutes. I dozed off at times, especially during the last half-hour. Yet each time my surgeon spoke to me I answered him and when he had finished he told me he was leaving and that the assistant doctor was taking over. I was amused as I watched the assistant doctor making neat fancy stitches and I complimented him.

This time I remembered my trip down by elevator. My husband and the nurse were waiting in my room. I talked incessantly about my wonderful experience in the operating room. Finally, the nurse gave me a sleeping pill to make sure I would get the important rest I needed.

I awoke in the night to another new experience, pain. A greedy, intense pain that left room for nothing else. The nurse hovered over me administering medications that brought intervals of relief throughout the endless night.

In the morning I felt as if I had been drawn through a knot-hole, but the pain had now become a tolerable, aching soreness. From my bed I watched the morning light break into a glorious sunrise. The peace I had experienced the morning before returned and with it a full-grown gratitude. I thought of the Twenty-third Psalm: "Yea though I walk through the valley of the shadow of death, I will fear no evil; for Thou art with me."

Repeatedly another thought came with force. Now God's healing power is at work in my body and there is no limit to His power. Two hours later, after my doctor's visit, with the help of my nurse, I slid to the floor from the high bed, walked across my room and back again. The first steps toward my complete recovery had been taken.

The remaining days of my hospitalization were like a vacation away from an exhausting schedule, in a room to myself where it was possible to think without interruptions.

There was pain and discomfort at intervals during the first

five days, but I soon learned that this was a necessary part of healing. But there was compensation in many other ways. I learned a new and wonderful kind of fellowship with the other patients on my floor. As each scheduled trip to the operating room came up we prayed. We laughed and griped a little too, over what seemed to us ridiculous hospital orders! We shared our get-well cards, our flowers, and introduced our families and friends to one another.

I have related this experience for several reasons. First, why did I stay awake when the anesthetist gave me additional drugs to keep me drowsy? When he called on me a week after the operation I had a chance to ask him about that.

"You had an overdose of what we call stimulus. *You willed to stay awake,*" he explained. "The mind has more than seventy-five per cent control over the body, you know."

I was aware now as never before of the power of the mind. The conscious mind was wonderful enough but how much more so was the unconscious mind, or the power of the soul.

Most of all, however, I learned again that God's peace does pass all human understanding and His healing power is available, if we are able with confidence to put our lives in His hands.

The day my doctor discharged me from the hospital he showed me my chart and remarked, "Your recovery was certainly normal in every respect, in fact it was super! Even your temperature remained normal every day of your recovery."

He then wrote the last entry: RECOVERY UNEVENTFUL!

II

* * *

Healing Through
the Church Service

Rise up, O Men of God!
Have done with lesser things;
Give heart and mind and soul and strength,
To serve the King of Kings.

Rise up, O Men of God!
The Church for you doth wait;
Her strength unequaled to her task;
Rise up and make her great!
—WILLIAM PIERSON MERRILL, 1867

PRELUDE: * GOD CAN HEAL YOU

A young couple entered St. Stephen's Episcopal Church in Philadelphia with their small son to attend a healing service. Andrew, clinging to his father's hand, was very ill. A year and a half before he had been a robust little boy. Suddenly without warning he became the victim of polio, then encephalitis (inflammation of the brain) set in. He had recovered somewhat but was left with a loss of hearing and the use of only one eye. Then he came down with a particularly virulent case of chicken pox. Finally an operation restored his hearing, but the vicious circle of disease left him weak, nervous and undernourished.

The father, holding Andy, and the mother knelt at the altar to await God's blessing. The rector, the Reverend Dr. Alfred Price, laid his hands upon the child and quietly prayed that God's healing power might enter the boy.

When the service was over the family found a nearby restaurant. At the table, his parents noticed that Andy sat up straight and that his eyes were sparkling. A moment later they were astounded as he asked the waitress, "Please may I have some spinach, a big hamburger on a bun and some mashed potatoes, with two glasses of milk?" The parents struggled with their tears of joy as they watched Andy eat as he had not done for nearly eight months. His mother, who had so often tried to tempt him with all kinds of desserts,

[21

now thanked God with all her being while she and her husband watched the boy finish his meal with pie and ice cream.

Out on the street again, Andy began to act more like his seven years. He insisted on walking ahead of his overjoyed parents. When they passed St. Stephen's all three of them stopped to look up at the great twin stone towers.

"Thank you, Daddy, for bringing me to this church. I feel good inside," was Andy's response.

In the weeks that followed the boy improved steadily and was able to undergo a long-hoped-for operation to restore the sight of his injured eye. The operation was a complete success. Today Andy is a healthy teenager, active in his home church and full of thanksgiving for God's healing power in his life.

1 * GOD MOVES IN MYSTERIOUS WAYS

The chimes of St. Stephen's Church reached me several blocks before I found its massive stone structure. The chimes rang out a favorite hymn:

> *God moves in a mysterious way*
> *His wonders to perform;*
> *He plants his footsteps in the sea,*
> *And rides upon the storm.*

The interior of the church, with its ebony-colored wood inlaid with mother-of-pearl, against a cream marble background, was far removed in appearance from the sensational places which I had come to associate in my mind with healing services.

There was no music or dim lighting, just the sunlight streaming through the beautiful rose window. The only sounds were made by the people who quietly filled the old-fashioned box pews. I found myself wishing there would be no healing service, only a worship service, the kind I understood.

Presently, a tall figure moved quietly down the aisle to take his place in the pulpit. After leading us in a brief prayer of praise and thanksgiving, the rector gave a short talk on divine healing. "God is on the side of health," he told us. "He is always longing to pour out His love and power through our prayers and intercession. God answers every genuine prayer according to the measure of our faith. If we create the proper conditions His power will flow through us healing every fiber, every tissue and every drop of blood.

"My friends," Dr. Price continued, "are you thinking: 'What can I do to be healed?' First you can relax, then with your spiritual imagination create in your mind a picture of the perfection in your body or mind which you crave. Put into your mind the right thoughts: thoughts of God's love; thoughts of His wholeness and healing which is already at work within you; thoughts of peace and confidence in Him. Appropriate God's power by faith, thanking Him with the realization that God has set free recuperative powers to heal and strengthen you."

Inviting those who wished to receive the laying-on-of-hands to kneel at the chancel, the rector went directly to the altar for consecration. Kneeling, he prayed: "O Lord, take my mind and think through it. Take my heart and set it on fire with Thy love. Take these hands and through them bring to these Thy suffering children, the fullness of Thy healing power. Amen."

Following the prayer some people quietly arose from their pews and became a part of the procession to the altar. Obviously they came from all stations of life. The suburbanite, the downtown rich and the poor, from every social stratum, from many callings and from none. Yet one felt a drawing together, a oneness arising out of their common urgency. A father and mother helped their crippled child, who walked between them. An unsteady and shabby figure propelled his sluggish body forward to sink upon his knees, his strength spent. In contrast, an immaculately dressed man glanced surreptitiously about him as if he feared he might be making a fool of himself.

The rector, quietly praying, placed his hands on each bowed head: "May the mercy of God and the love of our Lord Jesus Christ and the power of His Holy Spirit, which is here now, enter your soul, your mind and your body for healing. Amen."

The early Christians, meeting secretly in the catacombs, must, I thought, have experienced a oneness of spirit like this. I noted a new lift of the shoulders or a peaceful smile as those at the altar rose and returned to their pews, making room for others who waited to take their places at the chancel. Nothing spectacular happened at this service—that is, nothing seen by the naked eye—but I could no longer doubt that something did happen and that all who sought healing could be recipients of it. I wondered if this was not an example of what God could do with combined "prayer power," for even the persons remaining in the pews were bowed in earnest prayer.

It was evident to me that those who came to this service were not looking for an easy way out of their illness. If you have never done it before, it takes courage to kneel at an altar while others look on, to surrender all to God, within yourself, and to endeavor with a disciplined prayer life to serve others daily.

Near the close of the service Dr. Price again stood before the altar to read the names of those for whom prayer had been requested. He then pronounced the benediction. The healing service was over.

Though I shook hands with Dr. Price at the church door, I did not ask him for an interview. A week later, however, I phoned him and we made plans for a meeting. Ten years have slipped by since then, in which time Dr. Price and I have often discussed the subject of spiritual healing; I have attended many more healing services in his church and in scores of others. But I still remember how deeply moved I was that day at St. Stephen's after my first experience of a church healing service.

2 * TALL MAN OF GOD

Today St. Stephen's Church has become a spiritual oasis to thousands of people coming from all parts of the United States and Canada and even from many parts of the world. During frequent interviews with Dr. Price I learned how this church reached such a high point of helpfulness. Its rector had to endure many wrenchings of soul as he sought God's leading for a slowly dying city church to which he had been called from a flourishing suburban parish in Brooklyn. When he arrived at St. Stephen's, he discovered he had two parishes to serve.

"As I saw it," Dr. Price recalled, "the heart of the church lay nestled in the city streets while its great arms stretched out to the suburbs. How to serve my 'downtown parish,' as I have come to call it, was my real problem."

It was not the church's fault that the inevitable shifting from city to suburb that takes place in many large cities had finally caught up with St. Stephen's. For well over a hundred years this church was surrounded by elegant town houses of the prominent and well-to-do. Now it adjoins on one side a business section, where Philadelphia's largest department stores are located, and on the other a cheap rooming-house district.

"I prayed often," Dr. Price went on, speaking of his downtown parishioners: " 'Lord, show me how to help them find
You!' " We were both silent. As a member of the clerical
family I too knew that prayer, and I was also keenly aware of
the spirit of Alfred Price, which matched his huge, six-feet-
four-inch frame.

He turned to me with a smile. "And the Lord sure helped
me!" he chuckled. "God told me to visit my downtown parish,
all of it! I balked like mad. I argued with the Lord that it
was not considered respectable nowadays for a clergyman to
enter rooming houses to call on streetwalkers and drunkards,
but to no avail. I'll never forget my first call. I walked by the
nearest taproom a dozen times before I mustered enough
courage to go in. I put on a bold front but was quaking inside
as I made the first plunge. The bartender took one look at my
clerical vest and called the proprietor, who stuck his hand
out, saying, 'What can I do for you, Father?' "

" 'Oh, nothing,' I replied. 'Just came in to get acquainted.' "

Dr. Price told the owner of the taproom that he was the new
rector of the Episcopal church down the street and that if
he were ever needed he would be glad to help in any way he
could. He invited the man to bring his family to services at
St. Stephen's if he had no home church. He also told him
that although, as a clergyman, he did not approve of the
business the man was in he hoped nevertheless that they could
become friends.

The rector's less difficult visits around the business district
resulted in increased attendance at the church, especially at
daily noonday services, when sales girls, waitresses, file clerks,
secretaries and even busy brokers and professional people
paused to pray during the lunch hour. And gradually men and
women began to come from the rooming houses. Among
them were alcoholics, many of whom have since been healed
at St. Stephen's.

"Frankly, I had neither time nor energy to counsel all these
persons as it should be done," said Dr. Price. "I realized I

would have to be both psychiatrist and clergyman if I were to be of much help." Many new activities sprang up to meet the needs of those who now made St. Stephen's their church, and attendance at worship services was increasing. But this did not seem enough, as more and more people began to linger after services to talk with Dr. Price.

"I found so many ill, suffering from physical diseases, and with all kinds of problems. Some seemed to want to help themselves get well, while others only wanted to relieve their minds and souls periodically as they continued their dissipations. Yet it was not always easy for me to separate the two. All this time I think I was aware of a lack of a *vital spiritual awareness* in our church and I longed to find it, as a way to bring relief to these suffering people."

Then one day there came to Dr. Price's desk a pamphlet on divine healing. He had occasionally conducted a laying-on-of-hands service, especially during Lent and when those who were ill asked for it. Could this be the answer? There were so many who looked upon all faith healings as sensational and appealing only to the emotionally unstable.

"If I could be sure that this was what God wanted—but there was the possibility it might do more harm than good if hopes rose high and results did not measure up," Dr. Price told me.

With his Bible he wandered into the sanctuary, deep in thought, and slipped into one of the pews. This beautiful old church never ceased to inspire him. The rich heritage he felt was his while serving this church came through the lives of those who had worshiped here years before he was born. If they could talk to him would they approve of healing services? He glanced about at the many memorial plaques on the pews and then his glance fell upon the one where he sat. Surprised, he read: DR. S. WEIR MITCHELL. Surely *he* would approve, this great neurologist and pioneer of psychosomatic medicine. He recalled that this man had said, " 'Tis not the body but the mind is ill." The rector sat in the doctor's pew for a long time and read passage after passage on healing from the Bible.

Turning at last to a passage from James, which he had read many times to his congregation, he read again: "Is any sick among you? let him call for the elders of the church; and let them pray over him, anointing him with oil in the name of the Lord: And the prayer of faith shall save the sick, and the Lord shall raise him up: and if he have committed sins, they shall be forgiven him" (5:14-15). God had spoken to Alfred Price. He would begin a healing service as soon as possible. The Reverend Dr. Price rose from the doctor's pew a stronger man, a tall man of God.

3 * ARE THE SICK HEALED?

When Dr. Price first began his healing services they were far from popular. No more than eighteen persons attended.

"But having put my hand to the plow I could not turn back," Dr. Price told me, "nor did I want to, even though many of my well-meaning friends in the ministry were sure I was going off the deep end. It was inconceivable to them that in dignified, old St. Stephen's Church an Episcopal rector could be going into this healing business!"

Dr. Price drew his courage, however, from the Bible, basing his authority for what he was doing on Jesus' teachings. Christ's work as a teacher has received large recognition in the church, yet His ministry as a physician has been, since the fourth century, largely ignored or explained away as allegorical by believers, and denied as fictitious or mythical by unbelievers.

"Our work is based on the solid foundation of the Holy Scriptures, sound science, psychology and common sense."

said Dr. Price. "Christ was armed with boundless faith in God, and He knew that in answer to faith God stands ready to give all men not only forgiveness of sins, but the love, joy and self-control *that are the secret of health."*

Although the attendance at healing services for the first six months was not great the results were from the first remarkable. More and more people began phoning and writing Dr. Price about their recovery from illness.

"At first, I must confess, I was frightened of this power God had allowed to pass through my hands." Here Dr. Price paused, looked me straight in the eye and then continued: "I want you to understand and make clear as you write about our work that *I am not the healer but only the channel through which God sends His healing power.* This gave me cause for much soul-searching because I felt keenly my unworthiness and still do. Yet I came to accept the way in which I knew my Lord in His wisdom saw fit to use me."

The rector of St. Stephen's, having, once and for all, put his fears for this kind of a ministry into God's hands, was rewarded by the steadily growing results.

"I would like to ask you a question that many have asked me," I said. "Are people really healed in this church?"

Dr. Price smiled. "I'm always answering that one!" He rose from his desk and went to the file cases that lined the side wall of his study. Pulling out one of the drawers, he held up a folder filled with letters. "Judge for yourself," he said. "These cabinets are full of testimonial letters."

I have spent many hours over several years with these files and have taken many trips to interview the writers of these letters. I am convinced that people do receive God's healing gift in St. Stephen's Church.

Mr. A. M. wrote: "I stopped drinking the day you laid your hands on my head at the healing service. That was five years ago. I have been a changed man ever since. I know God gave me His gift of healing."

Another letter gave the experience of a business woman from the Boston area who had been sent by her firm to Philadelphia. Without warning, her leg began to swell. The doctor she found at once informed her that she had picked up a terrible infection which had spread rapidly. He made a reservation for her in a hospital and was afraid he would have to do an amputation the next day. She hobbled by St. Stephen's en route from her hotel to the hospital. On the sidewalk in front of the church she saw a sign announcing a healing service.

In the church a few minutes later she was much impressed as she sat listening to the rector tell how one could find healing through Christ. Later she wrote to Dr. Price: "As I knelt at the altar I felt an uplifting of my whole self. It was a wonderful feeling. When I reached the hospital I got into the bed reserved for me and thanked God for His love and goodness."

The next morning, when the doctor visited her and removed the bandages, he was surprised to find the infection healing. Two days later, still baffled, he discharged her as completely cured.

Some cures are as rapid as was this one, but many more have occurred gradually over a period of months and even years, as the following letter indicates:

Dear Dr. Price: It is the hour of your healing service as I write. I can picture you at the altar. I am joining in with you and all the others kneeling at the chancel rail. I am asking God to heal them as He did my daughter. We are thanking God constantly for His compassion and healing. For two years she suffered from a throat infection that made it so difficult to breathe that she was rushed to the hospital many times in order to save her life. After our visit to St. Stephen's she began to improve and found breathing much easier. We took her to a specialist for an examination and he found her throat "clean as a whistle" as he expressed it. She is not completely cured, but each day she is improving and we know she will be healed.

A stone-deaf woman heard the turning of the pages of the prayerbook as she sat in a pew during the healing service. It was the first sound she had heard in several years. She continued to come to the healing service each week and was able to tell Dr. Price three months later that she could now hear perfectly.

As a result of reading one letter to Dr. Price, I sought out Mrs. Sadie Desabaye, whose baby son was born with a club foot. The foot was almost completely imbedded in the leg. An eminent surgeon, after careful examination of X-ray pictures advised the mother not to expect a miracle but that if she massaged the leg, trying to stretch the tendons, it might help some.

"I believed that God wanted this baby to be like others and I knew He would heal Bobby," Mrs. Desabaye told me. "I massaged Bobby's leg every time I held him and I was sure it was growing normally. When he was two and a half years old the foot had grown out of the leg but had turned around. When Bobby finally started to walk he had great difficulty. He could not stand on the foot and began to drag it. I went to the doctor again and he gave me no hope at all this time."

Mrs. Desabaye had heard of Dr. Price's healing services at St. Stephen's, so she phoned him and asked if he thought she ought to bring Bobby to the service.

He answered, "By all means bring him." So she bundled him up and took him to the church.

"How did you feel as you took part in the service?" I asked.

"Oh, I was thrilled," she replied. "The church was so beautiful and quiet and Dr. Price's words seemed just for me. I just kept thanking God for guiding me there. Holding Bobby in my arms I went up to kneel at the altar rail with the others. When Dr. Price reached us he put one hand on Bobby's little head and one on mine. His touch was so gentle and I thought of Jesus and how He blessed little children. I felt reassured as a warm glow filled my heart."

The healing continued and Mrs. Desabaye told me that each day after that visit to the church, she could almost see the foot and leg straighten. Six months later Bobby was completely cured.

As I rose to leave, Bobby came in from school and his mother introduced him. He is now a friendly twelve-year-old boy, the picture of health with two strong legs and perfect feet. He often bicycles to and from school.

Approximately 40 per cent of those attending healing services at St. Stephen's are healed. The other 60 per cent might be labeled failures, failures in the sense that they have not received physical healing. The reasons are many and varied. Some reasons are not obvious and never will be, but many failures are accountable. Dr. Price told me about one man he wanted desperately to help.

He was an intelligent business executive fast becoming crippled with rheumatoid arthritis. He bemoaned the fact he had not been given the long-hoped-for promotion to the presidency of his firm. Next in line for the position, he had only received a kindly kick upstairs, with the title of associate vice-president, which meant just about nothing. Humiliating was the bitter fact that a younger man whom he had bossed for years was now his superior. The man had complained to Dr. Price, "I've prayed, but God is just not interested in me or my problem." The rector advised this man that he must learn to accept without bitterness his situation and then seek God's guidance. This advice went unheeded.

"I realized I could talk to him until doomsday but unless he did something about his problem my hands were tied," Dr. Price explained. "Unfortunately too many people seeking health expect a quick, easy way out. They hope to find a magic cure. This will never be found in my church. The desire for restored health must be secondary. It is evident to me, however, that those who come to our healing services regularly are not seeking another health cult, but are looking for an opportunity to understand the true meaning of Jesus' promise: 'I am come that they might have life and have it abundantly.' The theologian would say: 'To grasp the true meaning of the Incarnation.' "

The healing service is also recommended for the healthy person with problems other than illness. A middle-aged woman was able to overcome her unreasonable jealousy of her husband when at a healing service she suddenly realized her love was selfish and possessive. "Week by week I found strength to love unselfishly," she said, "until my husband began to notice the change. We are both happier than we ever dreamed we could be."

One young man told me, "I learned how to live with my mother-in-law and like it!"

All kinds of problems are solved at healing services, as one realizes that Jesus' promises are fulfilled if taken at their face value. A college professor learned how to relax in the middle of his lectures when he felt tension mounting. He said, "One day as I knelt at the healing service, too tired to care whether school kept or not, the revelation of Jesus' words, 'Come to me, all ye who labor and are heavy laden and I will give you rest' filled my mind and heart with a comfort and quiet joy. I suddenly knew I could work with ease instead of tension. 'Take my yoke upon you and learn of me' is no longer just a Bible verse. I have learned to recall this experience at moments when I need healing power."

Another woman told me she visited her psychiatrist twice a week until she attended a healing service. "Now I go to church and God is my psychiatrist," she added.

Supporting the healing ministry at St. Stephen's is a prayer fellowship of a hundred people who pray for the sick around the clock, twenty-four hours every day. In the chapters on prayer we will relate how this group operates and the results which it achieves.

Long ago it became humanly impossible for Dr. Price to fulfill all the prayer requests himself. He does, however, read every name before the altar during the closing prayer period of his healing service. But every day these prayer requests, which average about two hundred and are now placed in a special prayer box on the altar, are given special time and continued attention by the prayer fellowship.

Many letters come to Dr. Price thanking the prayer fellowship for its work. Mr. K., from Iowa, wrote:

> About three months ago I wrote asking prayer for our sister-in-law. Her doctors told her she had cancer. She had an operation and her doctor reported recently that she is completely well. She looks and feels wonderful, so please take her name off the prayer list. We can never thank God enough and you, and the prayer fellowship for the hours you spent in meditation for Rhoda. Through the pamphlets and literature you have sent me with your letters, I have come to understand man as a unit of body, mind and soul.

In addition to writing many pamphlets Dr. Price personally dictates thousands of answers to the letters he receives each year. On vacation he answers hundreds in longhand. Many of the letters are from those who have attended healing services in other churches across the country where he is invited to administer the laying-on-of-hands.

A businessman wrote Dr. Price:

> I attended your Healing Mission in St. John's Church in Washington, D.C. Ulcers were tearing me apart. What you said in your sermon helped me do some serious thinking. When I knelt at the altar and you placed your hand on my head, I realized that I was pushing people around, making them carry out what I thought my business needed. I asked forgiveness and help to change my attitude. As president and owner, I was the law, but at the next board meeting I listened to my associates,

then tried one new idea on which we all agreed. That was three months ago. My ulcers are completely healed, reports my doctor, and my business is on the upward trend, but most important, I have found real friendship and gained the respect of my employees.

1143355

Many letters report cures and also indicate a spiritual growth, ending on a note of praise and thanksgiving to God for His healing power:

Dear Dr. Price: On February seventh I had a minor operation and my surgeon discovered a small cyst which showed positive cancer cells. On February ninth we phoned you for prayers on my behalf. On February eleventh the surgeon did a mastectomy and to his great surprise not a single cell in that last removal of tissue showed any cancer whatever. He says I am one hundred percent cured! I am sure this is due to your intercessions and I am giving God all the credit for my healing. A.H.S.

Many individuals have dedicated themselves to Christ and their lives now show new purpose as they daily seek His guidance.

Many churches today are teaching that God does heal the body, physically and mentally, as well as spiritually, and they are seeing it happen. However, there are many angles to be considered and no one seeking healing through the laying-on-of-hands should expect results without some effort and discipline on his own part. Everyone seeking health must be willing to meet the necessary conditions.

I have asked Dr. Price to summarize some of these conditions. He gave me the following suggestions as aids to good health:

1. The patient must transfer his burden to God, believing that God can handle it perfectly. Healing does not take place in worried minds.

2. Tensions and resentment must be wiped out. God's love cannot flow through a spiteful spirit.

3. The patient must relax, rest assured in God's peace, confident that His will whatever it is will be best.

4. The patient should live expectantly knowing God's creative power is already at work. Thankfulness should be expressed for answered prayers. God should not be begged for healing.

5. Those trying to help should visualize the sick person as healthy. Picture him as he was before his illness.

6. Daily prayer and meditation is part of the therapy. The Gospels are to be studied and the life of our Lord should be familiar as well as the scriptures pertaining to healing.

7. The patient should be prepared to accept God's answer, remembering that His wisdom is best for your life and that His grace is sufficient for your every need.

Dr. Price firmly believes that many times God uses doctors and clergymen together in bringing about a cure. Therefore, he advises that the patient continue treatment with his doctor unless the doctor himself admits he can do no more for the afflicted one. He stresses the importance of striving to meet the necessary conditions through daily discipline, believing constantly that God *is* releasing His healing power.

These disciplines can be practiced anywhere, but Dr. Price feels it is beneficial for the sufferer to know he can attend his church regularly for healing and that prayer groups within the church are faithfully fortifying his faith with their prayers for his recovery. If one is physically unable to attend the church service, a friend or relative can receive the laying-on-of-hands for him.

Jesus told His disciples when He sent them out to establish the Christian church: "And into whatsoever city ye enter, and they receive you, eat such things as are set before you: And heal the sick that are therein, and say unto them, The kingdom of God is come nigh unto you" (Luke 10:8-9).

4 * THE BISHOP APPROVES

I felt I should attend one of the missions Dr. Price conducts in other cities. I learned that he had been instrumental in introducing healing ministries in the city of Pittsburgh, so I followed him there in March, 1953, during the Lenten season.

My first objective upon reaching the city was to gain an interview with Bishop Austin Pardue of the Episcopal Church, who because of his interest in spiritual therapy encouraged a healing ministry within the churches of the Pittsburgh area. Bishop Pardue had just returned from Korea, but I finally got word that he would see me for ten minutes.

Our interview lasted a good half-hour. To my question, "How did you become interested in spiritual healing?," he replied with the following story of an event which greatly influenced him as a young minister.

"While serving a small church in a Minnesota town," he said, "I had a friend, Bob Bowen, who was chief surgeon for the mining companies. He was a brilliant doctor who had refused to join the staff of a famous medical center in order to work in his beautifully equipped hospital on the Iron Range, where he ministered to men who worked in the open pit and underground mines, and to their families. He was a quiet man with a great sense of humor and whenever we could take time off, we would hunt and fish together. When I had a free night from my church duties, I would wander over to his hospital to listen as he talked with his patients. He believed in the mysteries of the power of healing. His faith in God's power was a strong link that bound us together. Often I would watch him finish a delicate surgical operation, then straighten up and say, 'Now it's up to Him.' "

One day Dr. Bowen called Austin Pardue to the hospital where a young woman they both knew was critically ill. Dr. Bowen had called in two prominent surgeons from other cities. Somehow he hoped they could save her life.

"When I arrived at the hospital," recalled Bishop Pardue, "Bob said, 'Austin, I'm turning her over to you until the consultation at six.' I went at once to the patient's room and found her in a coma. Standing beside her bed I weighed the facts: Here was an expectant mother who had been kept alive for three weeks through intravenous feeding. I prayed earnestly, then went in search of her husband whom I found in an extreme state of anxiety. I asked him to find an empty room somewhere in the hospital, and continue to repeat the Lord's Prayer."

Returning to sit by the woman's bed Austin Pardue continued to pray until at last she opened her sunken eyes. " 'Be still and know that I am God,' " he repeated. She tried to smile and closed her eyes again. Then the young minister printed these words in large letters and placed them by her bed, so she could see them whenever she opened her eyes. Pressing duties called him away from the hospital but he continued to pray for her, knowing God would let her see those words often.

"Two hours later I walked into her room and found her sipping tea and smiling at her husband," said Bishop Pardue. "Downstairs three surgeons were in consultation concerning an operation with a hundred-to-one chance for her survival. The operation never took place and that night the patient sat up and ate a full-course dinner. Her baby was born normally and is today a fine Christian mother herself."

"How do you account for this?" I asked.

"I don't," replied the Bishop. "I only know that the faith of a devoted doctor, coupled with that of the rest of us, did much to make her recovery possible."

I asked how the healing ministry in Pittsburgh had begun, and Bishop Pardue said, "I knew of Dr. Price's success in

his church in Philadelphia and a few years ago I decided to
send for him. Alfred Price graciously accepted my invitation
to spend a week with us during the Lenten season, at which
time he would administer the laying-on-of-hands at the noonday services in Trinity Cathedral. Each evening he would
assist a rector in conducting a healing service in the rector's
own church. Mornings would be given over to seminars for
the clergy, led by Dr. Price, where frank discussions on the
subject might be helpful." Bishop Pardue paused, then smiled
broadly. "And that did it!

"There is nothing new about the miracle of healing, you
know," he told me.

I spent the remainder of the morning reading material
Bishop Pardue had made available to me, until the chimes of
Trinity Cathedral next door reminded me of the noonday
services. I hurried out to find the city street filled with pre-
Easter shoppers and noonday strollers. It seemed as if most
of them were entering the cathedral with me.

Dr. Price led the Lenten service and at its conclusion invited the congregation to remain for the healing service. Several hundred people stayed to fill the chancel rail again and
again to receive the laying-on-of-hands.

It was two-thirty before the cathedral was empty and I
found Dr. Price in the vestry room, where he introduced me
to a radiant young couple. One year ago they had been deeply
troubled parents who had come to Dr. Price pleading for
help for their baby, who was now toddling happily around the
room as we talked.

"We brought our baby here to the vestry after the service
one year ago today," the father told me. "You see, she had
contracted a baffling disease and all the doctors had given up
hope for a cure."

"We were afraid to take her to the altar during the service
because she cried so much," explained the young mother.

"I was removing my vestments after the service when they
found me here," said Dr. Price.

"But he put them on again, not content to pray here in the vestry as we had asked him," the father added.

They had all gone back into the church, where Dr. Price took the baby in his arms, and carried her up to the altar; while the parents knelt at the chancel rail to pray, he asked God's healing love for this little life. The baby began to cry. Looking at me now through tears of gratitude the mother recalled, "Our baby cried even louder when Dr. Price gave her back to us, but he said, 'I feel certain that healing has already begun to take place and that in a few days your baby will be cured.'"

"She cried for three days," continued the father, "and then she stopped and we knew she was healed!" And I knew it too as I watched her for a moment and listened to the chattering baby sounds as she investigated every corner of the vestry room.

That night Dr. Price invited me to go with him to St. Stephen's Episcopal Church in Wilkinsburg, a suburb of Pittsburgh, where he was to hold a healing service. At the close of the service a period of fellowship followed in the social hall. Dr. Price and the rector of the church, Dr. A. Dixon Rollit, were most helpful in giving me an opportunity to interview people who had received healing through that church.

George Pressley, a successful middle-aged businessman, together with his gracious wife told me of his complete recovery from migraine headaches even when the prescribed narcotics offered little relief.

"First I want to explain that we were acquainted with suffering long before the headaches of several years ago," Mr. Pressley began. "The night before my graduation from the University of Pennsylvania I was involved, with some classmates, in an automobile accident which for me resulted in a fractured skull, broken jaw, broken kneecaps, mangled hands, cut eyeball and a crushed larynx box. I overheard the surgeon remark that my case was hopeless, but I lived on even though I prayed for death. Those who loved me prayed for my recovery. One of these was my clergyman uncle, who finally got through to me that I must have faith in prayer, for he believed that it was God's will that I should live."

I was astonished as George Pressley talked, for he was a picture of health and was certainly in full command of all his faculties. His next statement was overwhelming. "Successful operations one after another pieced me together except for the larynx, which was not completely repaired. However after a long, hard try I learned to talk with my diaphragm." To me his speech sounded no different from mine.

He enjoyed good health for several years, until headaches began to plague him and he found himself in one hospital after another—Philadelphia, Baltimore, Harrisburg and Pittsburgh—for tests and treatments.

"From the specialists in these medical centers I got all kinds of reasons for the headaches. One said they were the result of the fractured skull. The second hospital treated me for migraines, the third for internal injuries and the fourth for hypertension, but always the prescribed treatment failed."

"Two years ago, our rector, Dr. Rollit, had begun to hold healing services in our church," explained Mrs. Pressley, "and during the Lenten season invited Dr. Price to hold services as he did tonight. I tried to interest George in attending but he didn't believe in this kind of 'quick magic,' as he called it."

"Well, you see, I was a bit skeptical of healing services because of the methods used by a certain evangelist here in Pittsburgh," her husband added. "But when my wife told me that Dr. Price, also a graduate of the University of Pennsylvania, was having great success with his healing ministry in Philadelphia, I decided to go just to see what an alumnus of my school had to offer!"

George Pressley was impressed with the ring of conviction that is so much a part of Dr. Price's services and has impressed so many other skeptics. When the invitation was extended to go to the altar rail he joined the procession.

"I was deeply moved, but nothing happened in the way of relief from these headaches which hit me periodically," he recalled. "My wife did not have to ask me to go with her, though, to Dr. Rollit's weekly healing services, which began with communion and followed with the laying-on-of-hands. One day a few weeks after Dr. Price's visit, while I was kneeling at the chancel rail during a healing service, the thought came to me that the headaches were a direct result of my liver. The next day I went to a doctor who verified this thought. He has been able to prevent these severe headaches through medication for the liver condition and through diet."

When I asked George Pressley to sum up his thoughts regarding spiritual healing, he said, "I believe that God used medical science and faith to bring about my recovery. I feel that spiritual healing should be practiced in every Protestant church. Protestantism should rise up to meet this need and I, personally, am very grateful to my church, to my rector and to Dr. Price for the help they made available to me."

I talked also with a steelworker I will call Henry Walker, who had suffered an accident while working at the mill. His pelvis was so badly crushed that he was told by doctors he would never walk again. During his six months in the hospital he was placed on the critical list with no hope of recovery. Dr. Rollit prayed for him. After six months he was released from the hospital and returned to his home an invalid. Prayers were said for him in the church each week at the healing service.

"As you can see I am now walking," Henry Walker told me. "A few weeks after my return home I was able to get out of my wheelchair and attend the healing services myself. I know God's healing power can be released in people today, if we are willing to put ourselves in his hands."

Mrs. Jane B., a pleasant young woman in her thirties, told me she had had trouble with her eyes. Vision in the left eye grew hazy and the medical report showed a growing cataract. An operation would eventually be inevitable.

"I prayed for healing, releasing my problem to God, determined to give him a chance while I waited for the operation." Jane said. She read daily some of Dr. Price's pamphlets on healing which she had received at one of the healing missions he had conducted in Pittsburgh. She attended the laying-on-of-hands each week in the Wilkinsburg Episcopal church, because her own Methodist church did not have healing services. Two months later while worshiping in her own church one Sunday morning the haze seemed to be lifting from her eye. She went to see her doctor that week and he noted it was much improved. "Whatever you are doing," he told her, "keep it up." In another month her eyesight was completely restored.

Not only does healing take place in the body but, more important, in the soul, where the real change takes place; and the renewal of the soul is after all the duty of the church. An accomplished woman who had been healed of cancer summed it up for me beautifully.

"Not a religious person," she said, "I nevertheless felt the need for communion the night before my operation. During the communion given to me by the hospital chaplain, a peace I can never fully describe came over me. I knew Christ for the first time in my life. When you have found Him as sincerely as I did that night, you have Him forever!"

5 * A FAITH STRONGER
       THAN STEEL

I often think of Pittsburgh as "The City of God" because I have never known any other city with so many healing services and prayer fellowships and such a large number of people who take spiritual healing as a matter of course. Numerous churches in this great city are responding to a faith in God which is far stronger and more powerful than its most important product—steel.

In many denominations throughout Pittsburgh the ad-ministering of the laying-on-of-hands is a regular part of the churches' program. I have visited many of these churches during my several journeys to Pittsburgh.

I found a vital and large healing service at St. Peter's United Church of Christ, where the Reverend Doctor Richard Rettig is pastor. Dr. Rettig's conception of a heal-ing ministry follows closely the beliefs and methods of Phil-adelphia's Dr. Price. Unlike most churches, which began the healing ministry in an effort to help the sick, this church became interested because of a direct answer to the prayers of its pastor for one of his parishioners. Dr. Rettig introduced me to Howard Lambert, a young married man, the father of several children, saying, "This is the young man who in-directly is largely responsible for awakening us to the fact that healing services in our church could be invaluable."

Howard began to tell me his story: "One April evening just before dinner, my wife sent me to the store for ice cream. The roads were half wet from a drizzling rain and I was in a bad mood, tired and hungry, and driving too fast. A child dashed in the street in front of my car. To avoid her I crashed into a telephone pole."

Later Howard found himself in a hospital with several doctors and nurses working over him to stop the bleeding. Gashes on his head required one hundred stitches. His shoulder was dislocated, but all this was nothing compared to the condition of his right leg. The femur (the big bone from the hip to the knee) was badly broken.

"After four months in the hospital," continued Howard, "the doctors placed a seventy-five-pound cast on my leg and sent me home. I was to report back to the hospital every month for X-ray treatment. Three months later I was in the hospital again. The doctors told me that my leg had become ulcerated and the bone would not knit. Their only solution was an operation to insert a silver bar from my hip to the knee, which would leave me crippled for life. This was the blackest period of my life and I was sure I would never be useful again."

Dr. Rettig visited Howard regularly during his illness and was deeply concerned for this young man. He knew that Howard would soon have to give his consent or refusal on the operation. Dr. Rettig had long believed in spiritual healing and made it a habit to spend several mornings a week in prayer for the sick of his congregation.

"I can never explain the feeling that came over me one morning as I prayed for Howard," Dr. Rettig told me. "Somehow I knew a miracle was in the making, for a wonderful feeling possessed me. I was certain that something unusual had happened or was about to happen."

That same morning Howard, lying in his hospital bed, was debating what he should do concerning the operation. Should he give his permission for it? If he refused, would he die slowly and painfully from infection?

"Many thoughts on healing by prayer which my pastor had given me filled my mind," Howard recalled. "I knew Dr. Rettig and the whole congregation were praying for me, especially every Sunday during the morning service. Maybe it was time for me to do some real praying, too! I began to see that I had never taken my faith seriously. So now I asked God to forgive me and help me to understand His way for my life. One thing I did know; only God could help me to walk again. Slowly the thought that God could do it possessed me."

Then one day quite unexpectedly Howard was aware of a pricking sensation in his injured leg, which had been numb for months. Hope surged within him as he tried doggedly to move his limb. Again and again he tried and gradually the determination to stand on his feet became an obsession.

At that moment Dr. Rettig arrived at the hospital. Entering Howard's room, he stopped spellbound, for there stood the young man who had not walked for seven months, smiling at him triumphantly, holding on to the bed for support. Tears of grateful joy ran down Dr. Rettig's face.

Howard told me of his feelings at that never-to-be-forgotten moment. "That was the beginning of my healing," he said. "But something far more important happened to me as I stood looking at Dr. Rettig. I realized *how much he cared for me* and I understood for the first time *how much God loved me, too.* I not only found healing—I found God!"

Not long after this momentous day the doctors decided to grant Howard's request to go home for a while, with the reservation that he was to return in three months for the recommended operation.

At home Howard prayed and worked. He concentrated on getting well by moving his leg every day until he could lift it straight up in the air. Then he tried walking. Soon he was able to enroll for a course in radio and television technique, partly by mail. At first the Pittsburgh college refused him entrance because they required all examinations to be taken in the classrooms. Would he be physically able to meet the requirements? With great faith, Howard was able to assure the professors that he would be there when that time came. Four months after leaving the hospital Howard hobbled downtown to take his finals, which he passed with straight A's.

"Then I went back to the hospital for the check-up, determined to talk the doctors out of the operation," Howard said. "But when they removed the cast my doctors were amazed to see the healthy condition of the flesh where the ulcerous area had been. Further examinations and X-ray pictures proved that new bone had actually grown exactly where the surgeon had planned to insert the silver bar. The doctors had no explanation to offer and one jokingly said, 'Well, Howard, you have cheated us out of an operation.' But Dr. Rettig and I know that God healed me."

It is understandable then that at St. Peter's United Church of Christ healing services are now an important part of its ministry. Dr. Rettig told me that his own spiritual life and that of the church membership has been strengthened in a remarkable way. Pastors engaged in a healing ministry are keenly aware of this added blessing.

"Spiritual maturity is bound to result," Dr. Rettig explained, "when we forget ourselves, while earnestly praying for others. The results of God's power at work, not only bring to us a deep sense of gratitude but a feeling of unworthiness and a desire to surrender ourselves to our Lord."

Many people are healed of all kinds of ailments, even supposedly incurable diseases, in Dr. Rettig's weekly healing services, and in every church where a healing ministry is offered, this is also true.

"When I first became convinced of our need for this kind of service," Dr. Rettig said, "I met with Dr. Price, who took time to help me. I will always be grateful to him and to the Episcopal church for their pioneering work in this important ministry."

I have found a growing interest among ministers and their congregations in many churches across our country and have read of successful work in other countries. An increasing number of churches are realizing that more of the church's program must be devoted to the sick and desperately troubled people of today's world.

I have never met a minister who was not deeply concerned with the spiritual health of every person in his parish. He believes in the redemptive power of God and knows the marvelous ways in which it transforms the life of man. He is, therefore, not against healing by faith, although he is often unjustly accused, but he is cautious of some of our present-day methods of healing and the beliefs and claims of some groups. He knows it is not wise to rush into a healing ministry without giving much time to prayerful meditation and thoughtful study of the whole field.

The following suggestions, which were given to me by members of the clergy now engaged in weekly healing services, may be helpful:

1. Begin by reading: *Psychology, Religion and Healing,* by Leslie D. Weatherhead, the well-known English minister. This many feel is most helpful because it is written by a pastor and is a result of his study and personal experience in the field of psychology and spiritual healing during his active ministry. Simultaneously read the Bible, especially the sections dealing with what Jesus said and did about healing the sick.

2. Visit churches engaged in healing services such as the laying-on-of-hands, prayer groups, church clinics and pastoral counseling. If the minister decides to begin a healing ministry he should be sure that his temperament is suited to a service of this type. Some ministers find they are *not* of the right temperament to give the laying-on-of-hands. In larger churches one of the assistant ministers may be called upon for this service while another minister may do the counseling. Whatever approach is used the minister should be prepared and feel completely sure that this is God's leading for him.

3. When the minister is ready through his own study and meditation he should acquaint his congregation with the subject through preaching and teaching, or a few interested members might study with the minister using the above suggestions.

It may not be quite so easy to believe in the power of our Lord to heal today as it was when Jesus performed these miracles, but as more and more people are seeking health for a useful life, it becomes the duty of the church to open its mind and heart to the healing power of prayer not yet fully explored.

III

* * *

*Healing Through
the Power of Prayer*

1 * TWENTY-FOUR-HOUR
PRAYER VIGIL

Thousands of churches have established prayer groups. The idea is by no means a new one. It began in the early Christian Church as described in the book of Acts. Meeting secretly in the catacombs, under threat of death, even by torture, the early Christians did not fail regularly to seek strength together through prayer.

Today, a great resurgence of these groups is fast producing, once again, the foundation on which the church grows. The lives of individuals are changed for the better because of the power released by these groups. Abundant life is ours today—more surely than ever when two or three gathered together turn in full surrender to our Lord, Jesus Christ.

For instance, the secret behind the success of St. Stephen's Episcopal Church in Philadelphia and its healing ministry is the earnest practice of prayer, not only by individuals seeking healing but by the regular intercessory prayers of the St. Stephen's prayer fellowship, mentioned earlier.

This fellowship is made up of a group of over one hundred carefully selected persons many of whom have experienced healing themselves. This unusual prayer fellowship meets regularly once a month with Dr. Price, for inspiration, meditation and for the purpose of bringing the prayer list up to date. The prayer list contains over four hundred names of those who have recently attended a healing service or who request prayers as they lie in bed, at home or in the hospitals. The fellowship prays in turn for all these, regularly every day and night, twenty-four hours around the clock, as long as their names remain on the prayer list. The members each select the one hour most convenient to them and devote that time to the names on the prayer list. They seldom know the person for whom they pray.

Those who are sick come to depend on the prayers of the fellowship and many letters come to Dr. Price expressing gratitude and reports on the condition of the sick one.

"It is so comforting to know that as I lie here in the hospital that all day long and late into the night one hundred people are praying for me by name. I know I have nothing to fear and that I will soon be well again."

A man fighting paralysis wrote: "I will be reading my Bible on Thursday during your laying-on-of-hands service. Continue to pray for me. Your prayer fellowship is pulling me through."

"Healthy minds are necessary to healthy bodies," declares Dr. Price. "Religion creates the healthy attitude of mind. It does it better than anything else I know. It brings peace, confidence, assurance, deep and abiding trust in a power greater than ourselves, ever ready and waiting to help us. *Prayer is a means of approach to that power.*"

Dr. Price always has several letters to read to the members of the prayer fellowship at their regular meeting. For example:

> Last spring I wrote to you requesting prayers for my little niece, Barbara Jane. At that time she was desperately ill in the Children's Hospital with meningitis. I attended the healing service later and heard her name included in the prayers. I am happy to inform you she is now entirely well and we all want to thank you for your kindness. I am sure the prayers of your fellowship were heard.

The prayer fellowship began in a natural and quiet way in the spring of 1949. As the healing ministry grew and the number of prayer requests began piling up on Dr. Price's desk, Dorothy Kohl, a member of his church, came to him one day offering to pray regularly for the sick.

"I feel extremely grateful for my own healing," Dorothy told me when I went to her for the history of the prayer fellowship. "You see, I had been suffering from a severe case of shingles and my doctor said this condition would continue three months or more because there were many shingles under the skin that had to come out."

In desperation she went to see Dr. Price, who counseled her to relax, to let go, and to ask God to take over her problem. They prayed together and when she was leaving, Dr. Price told her cheerfully, "By Christmas your shingles will be gone." Three days later, on Christmas morning, Dorothy found that they had completely disappeared.

Dorothy's earnest desire to help Dr. Price in prayer led to the gradual development of the St. Stephen's Prayer Fellowship. She began meeting with two other friends to pray for the sick who sought help in the church. Then she and her two friends started praying with Dr. Price, believing God would direct others to become a part of this fellowship.

"It was amazing how God sent others to us," she said. "A doctor came when a patient of his was healed. Today he is still a member of our prayer fellowship."

At present there are ten doctors, many nurses, business executives, lawyers, television personalities, housewives, sales clerks and many others who count it a great privilege to serve God one hour, either through the day or night, as a member of the prayer fellowship.

"I had a great need for prayer in my own life and for a member of my family," a business executive and a member of St. Stephen's Prayer Fellowship told me when I called on him in his office. "One day I left my office in desperation," he said, "and walked to St. Stephen's Church to pray. I'd heard so much about the healing service and was told prayers were really answered there."

This man found peace from anxiety and his prayers were answered in a way he had not thought possible. Soon he too offered to pray for others. Now he conducts daily prayers in his office with his secretary and other employees.

"Although my employees are of different faiths, there is complete harmony as we pray for a good working relationship together and for their families and friends in need and for a better world."

One of the fellowship members I have come to know is Mrs. Lois Thomson, a widow, and a member of St. Stephen's who has faithfully served her church for many years. Dr. Price was glad to enlist her services to assist him in answering the hundreds of letters he receives every week. There is much routine work to this job, for long ago Dr. Price was compelled to draw up three types of form letters which are sent initially in order to classify the prayer requests. In many cases these are followed by personal letters which Dr. Price dictates to his secretary, Joseph Leeds, and to Mrs. Thomson.

While Dr. Price is away on his various healing missions, Lois Thomson reads every letter that arrives as if it were from a personal friend. One day she revealed to me how grateful she was for what this position has meant to her.

"No amount of money could give me the lift I get from reading these letters," she admitted. "If I'm depressed I just read a few letters and my burdens disappear. Even the routine part of the work is made easier with the thought that each envelope I address is giving some poor soul a chance to find God and a better life." As a member of the prayer fellowship she prays for one hour every day, at 8 A.M.

Lois has received God's gift of healing. For many years she had been troubled with a sacroiliac displacement. One day when she returned home from a healing service, she felt God's presence like a quiet joy. Although it was late in the afternoon and not her regular morning time to pray, she felt so grateful that she sat down to thank God and, picking up the prayer list, she prayed for the sick. Just as she finished praying, she felt the bones in her back move gently into place. It is difficult to realize that Lois once suffered from this painful back condition. She is now a radiantly healthy and happy person.

In St. Stephen's Prayer Fellowship one finds the same quality of faith we read about in the Acts when Peter raised Dorcas from the dead. It requires no stretch of the imagination to see all Dorcas' friends of the village uniting their prayers with Peter's, as they waited outside her door. The compassion and deep love these early Christians possessed, linked with their firm belief that God could and would restore Dorcas through Peter, was the generating power their faith released. Imagine the joy that filled each one waiting outside that chamber when Peter called them and presented Dorcas alive!

With one hundred persons having learned through suffering and disciplined lives how to release God's power for others, it is not presumptuous to say: no wonder so many are healed through the healing ministry of St. Stephen's Church.

2 * THE SCHOOL OF PRAYER

I was in Pittsburgh on an assignment for *Guideposts*. I had finished my work and was packing when the telephone rang. It was the hotel's desk clerk informing me that my flight to Philadelphia would be delayed several hours because of weather conditions. Nothing is more depressing than hanging around a hotel when one is eager to get home. I opened my briefcase, and began sorting the mass of material I had collected during the week.

I had recently finished reading Helen Shoemaker's book, *The Secret of Effective Prayer*, and I remembered that her husband, Dr. Samuel Shoemaker, was rector of the Calvary Episcopal Church in East Liberty, a suburb of Pittsburgh. For a moment I thought of phoning Mrs. Shoemaker, but I had the notes on my interviews before me, and I became engrossed in reliving the talks I had just had with people who had shared their exciting faith experiences with me. However, like a needle caught in a record groove, the thought persisted: "Phone Helen Shoemaker."

Finally, I put the call through and shortly I was hearing Helen's cheerful "hello." She was delighted to know that I liked her book and was recommending it to our prayer fellowships in Philadelphia. Then she asked me how I happened to be in Pittsburgh. The next thing I knew I was in a taxi on my way out to see her.

We hit it off right away. We were both wives of ministers, both mothers and writers, and had the fellowship of our Lord and His work at heart. We talked animatedly. Then for a moment we became strangely silent, both possessed with the same unexpressed thought.

"I wonder why God brought us together?" I asked.

"That's what I've been thinking," Helen replied. Then she laughed and said, "But never fear; He will let us know when He is ready."

Dr. Shoemaker came in the room as I got up to leave. Suddenly Helen's face brightened.

"Maybe God wants you to write about our School of Prayer," she said. Dr. Shoemaker agreed. "You'll find plenty to write about in these prayer groups," he said.

I don't know why but I knew at that moment that they were right, although it then seemed impossible because of my other writing commitments. Upon my return home, Len LeSourd, my *Guideposts* editor, phoned for a report. I found myself telling him about my meeting with Helen.

"Sounds like a good story," he said. "Why not look into it some more and report back?"

Letters flew between Helen and me. Four weeks later I was

in Pittsburgh again to learn about a church which is directly responsible for over two hundred prayer-fellowship groups in and around Pittsburgh.

Helen met my train at dawn on a wet and cold Monday. We had breakfast together in the Shoemakers' beautiful old rectory across the street from the great Gothic church. Helen gave me a briefing on the history of the prayer groups which functioned under her enthusiastic guidance. I wanted to know first why they began and how.

Samuel and Helen Shoemaker believe that a wide gap exists between private prayer and public worship. "This is a phase of Christianity long neglected in many Christian churches," Helen said. "There is a real need for the small fellowship group, or prayer study group, where individuals can study the Bible together, pray together, and discover Christ's call to them together."

This devoted rector and his wife realize that even in busy church groups people are lonely and need a fellowship deeper than that of working together on some common project.

"You see," Helen explained, "many need to feel that other people will help them and stand by them, over and above the call of duty. That is why the thoughtful, unhurried reading of the Bible in small groups is important and intercessory prayer is absolutely necessary if spiritual maturity and healings are to result."

When Dr. Samuel Shoemaker came to Calvary Church in 1952, he began his crusading with small groups of young couples in the privacy of his book-lined study. Here he guided those who wanted to face their own lives honestly, and endeavor to learn how to become Christians.

Helen Shoemaker found God leading her to larger groups as she accepted a growing number of invitations to address all kinds of church and civic groups on prayer and prayer groups. Sensing a hunger and earnest longing for a richer prayer experience on the part of so many church people, she set up a six-week school, with the efficiency of an expert executive.

The response exceeded her greatest expectations. People came from all parts of Pittsburgh and its environs to learn how to begin prayer fellowships in their own churches. Meanwhile the women of Calvary Church, who had often experienced the power of prayer, gratefully stood by their rector's wife, helping her organize more prayer groups within the church.

The first School of Prayer was held in Calvary Church in January, 1953. In three years the attendance rose from one hundred and five to four hundred people. That first year eleven prayer groups were formed. At present there are more than two hundred, located in churches of various denominations within the city of Pittsburgh and outlying towns within a radius of fifty miles. For the past seven years as many as one thousand prayer-group members have attended the September prayer-group reunions, where such eminent men of prayer as Dr. Elton Trueblood and Dr. John S. Bonnell have addressed them.

The afternoon of my arrival I walked with Helen through a downpour of rain from the Shoemaker rectory to the church across the street to attend the School of Prayer.

"You can't expect many to come out in weather like this," I commented.

"You'll see," Helen laughed.

As the strong winds whipped my umbrella about, I saw a number of cars pulling up to the church door and one after another letting out their passengers, who hurried inside out of the rain. Ten minutes later Helen Shoemaker stood before an audience of some three hundred women who listened spellbound for a full hour, while she challenged them to self-disciplined lives of prayer.

Later she led a discussion period on how to interest others in becoming a part of a prayer study group. Many questions were raised and answered.

"Why isn't daily personal prayer and divine worship on Sunday enough?" asked a woman.

"Jesus did not consider it enough," replied Mrs. Shoemaker. "It is true that He said, 'When thou prayest, enter into thy closet, and when thou hast shut thy door, pray to thy Father which is in secret.' But He also said 'If two of you shall agree on earth as touching anything that they shall ask, it shall be done for them of my Father.' So you see, Jesus told us to do both and not either/or."

The next question came from a young minister who was serving his first church. I had met him and three of his church members before the meeting. "As you know, Mrs. Shoemaker, we have just formed a prayer group, thanks to your interest," he said. "But I have so much to learn about the power of prayer." Then turning with an appreciative smile to those who accompanied him he said, "Without the help of these three ladies I'd be at sea most of the time. The sharing of their prayer experiences with me has enriched my life. We came here today to learn how to pray for the healing of the sick. Suppose the one for whom we pray is not healed?"

The interest this question created was evidenced by the intense stillness of the room just before Mrs. Shoemaker replied. "There are many reasons why people are not healed and there is not time now to discuss them all, but since you came here to learn how to pray for the sick, first let me suggest that you look over the book table before you leave. There you will find material which deals with this question. One of the important reasons why prayers for healing are not answered is that possibly our anxiety and fear are stronger than our faith in God's love and His power to act. This blocks God's power."

Although the School of Prayer was not begun primarily for the healing of the afflicted, it is inevitable that one of the by-products of a prayer group which includes prayer for the sick should be healings.

Regarding the power of prayer to heal the sick, Helen Shoemaker said, "Christ never promised us release from suffering but He put into our hands His weapon of prayer and promised that if we use it, all things are possible."

Mrs. Shoemaker has written in *Power Through Prayer Groups* and *The Secret of Effective Prayer* of the many occasions she has had to test this promise.

3 * PRAYER FELLOWSHIPS HEAL

The slogan "Prayer changes things" needs no proving at Calvary Church. I talked with many people of all ages who were willing to share the results of their participation in a prayer group if it might help others to find the same joyful experience.

My second morning in Pittsburgh Mrs. Samuel Poorman called at my hotel to drive me to the prayer group of which she is a member. Her smile was warm and friendly.

"My name is Anne," she said. "I will be glad to help you in any way you wish while you are here."

"Well, let's start with you," I said.

"Good," she laughed. "However, nothing worth printing happened to me, I'm afraid. I just thought I was a pretty good church member until I got into a prayer study group and then I began to see I was living a very materialistic life. For the first time I *really* began to be interested in people. Empathy is the word to describe it, I think. Before I joined a group I was interested in people to a degree but I wouldn't have thought of spending a whole day—or even an hour—in prayer for someone in need. Now it is a joy to be a channel through which God can work even though it requires constant discipline, as I learn how to surrender to Christ more completely every day."

Arriving at Mrs. R.'s attractive apartment we met with nine other women who echoed the fine spirit I found in Anne. Mrs. R. was the prayer leader and at 10:30 A.M. she opened the fellowship with prayer; then the Bible-study period followed, with frequent use of several commentaries and *The Interpreter's Bible.* The group talked together concerning the meaning of the Scriptures, asking questions, which were assigned to some member of the group for the next week's meeting if they could not be answered. Intercessory prayer for the sick and troubled closed the hour.

Most of the eight groups I visited followed this pattern, more or less, and the members told me many stories of answered prayers. One of the women's groups was asked by the Council of Churches of Pittsburgh to prepare a pamphlet on the technique of the prayer group, under the title "Try Prayer."

"We worked long and hard on it," Mrs. T. told me over the lunch table. "We not only worked on the technique of organization, the experiences to be reached and the resulting rewards, but we were eager to present the pitfalls that prayer groups should avoid: a holier-than-thou attitude, or a small group becoming exclusive with only best friends; guarding against centering prayers on members and their interests, forgetting world-wide needs. Also we cautioned against confusing sociability with prayer fellowship and warned against groups becoming too large. The training of leaders is important for those interested in forming new groups."

I asked Mrs. L., one of the three women who wrote the pamphlet, "Try Prayer," for a statement on the results she thought most rewarding.

"Oh, there are so many rewards," she answered, "such as learning how to pray. I remember when we began that no one could pray aloud and we sat in silence. Then some of us

found courage and read our carefully written prayers. But as
the weeks slipped by we became aware of God's presence and
spontaneous prayers burst from us. Now we all pray! Prayer
group members grow closer to each other and God through
the study of the Bible. We are bound together by our mutual
growing love for Christ, our Lord."

Another woman from one of the groups I attended told me
of the marvelous healing of an alcoholic member of her
family. "Nothing helped until the prayer group began praying
for him. Then gradually the cure took place. I am convinced
that prayer is the greatest power on earth," she declared.

During the Coffee Hour after Sunday morning service I
met another member of one of the prayer groups, Mrs.
Marjorie Bean, and her husband, Henry.

"Mrs. Shoemaker tells me you have had a remarkable experience," I said, by way of introduction.

"We certainly have," she replied. "All our married life we
seemed to have our share of troubles and we worried through
them as a lot of people do. Now we have learned that real
faith brings confidence and trust beyond our own power.
Henry was very ill this past spring. We now realize it was
largely his own fault for trying to burn the candle at both
ends. In addition to carrying on his business, he also insisted
on accepting many singing engagements in his spare time,
even when he was suffering from a severe case of flu.

"Ultimately he found himself in the hospital with acute
rheumatoid arthritis. The pain was intense. I blamed myself
and felt I had failed in my duties as a wife. He had pains all
over his body but one knee joint drove him nearly crazy. We
were beside ourselves with worry.

"One of the Calvary prayer groups prayed for us and our
beloved rector, Dr. Shoemaker, called at the hospital to see
Henry, who by that time was in such pain that he did not
care whether he lived or died. I am sure Dr. Shoemaker was
sent by God. At the conclusion of his short visit, he asked
the Lord to heal the affected knee joint. He told me to lay

my hand, with his, on Henry's knee, telling me that God's power, in answer to our prayers, would flow down our arms and into the swollen knee. We prayed earnestly, believing that nothing is impossible with God."

Three hours later Marjorie Bean walked into her husband's room to find him so changed she was astounded. Sitting up in bed, he cheerfully reported the pain had almost disappeared. Marjorie noted with joy that the swelling had gone down considerably. He continued to recover speedily, to the amazement of his doctors.

"We no longer worry about our problems," Marjorie went on, "but constantly believe that in time they will be solved as long as we try to help others and endeavor to live consecrated lives." Henry Bean nodded in agreement and added that he has continued in the best of health.

I was looking forward to meeting Mrs. O., for many people had spoken to me of her faith. She greeted me graciously from a wheelchair. Here was an unusual woman, in whose face I saw a reflection of spiritual acceptance mingled with her suffering.

"Helen Shoemaker asked me to visit you," I said. "She told me you have experienced the power of prayer in a wonderful way."

"Yes, I have." She spoke softly as she told me how prayer had saved her life. "It was a glorious day in October, 1954, when I drove slowly by beautiful old Calvary Church. I had just been to my own church where that day we began a prayer group fashioned after the one I had attended at Calvary. I thought of Helen Shoemaker who had first interested me in prayer groups. I was thanking God for what this meant to me in the way of spiritual growth when I looked up—and there was Helen waving to me from the sidewalk. I pulled to the curb and she climbed in my car. I remember saying, 'Helen, my prayer for myself is that God may use me.' Little did I realize how that prayer would be answered."

One week later Mrs. O. drove off with her sister for a holiday in Virginia. The weather was bad but they were eager to begin their trip, so they ignored the advice of the family that they wait until conditions improved. In the early afternoon they left the turnpike and pushed on through driving rain over a twisted and fog-bound road. Suddenly their car skidded and they had a sense of flying off into space.

Mrs. O. continued her story: "I heard my sister, who was driving, say in a desperate voice, 'Oh, my God! Oh, my God!' Much later I learned that our heavy car had locked brakes, raced at terrific speed over tall, rain-beaten grass across a field, and crashed into a farmhouse. Our car was virtually demolished but we were still alive. I was unconscious but my sister, in spite of a broken leg and cut face, was able to direct our rescue."

In a critical condition Mrs. O. was taken by ambulance to a small medical center ten miles away. Miraculously just one pint of her type of blood was at hand; this sustained life in her broken body for another thirty-mile drive over two mountains, through fog and rain, to the nearest hospital. An orthopedic surgeon of superior skill, together with his assistants, spent many hours trying to save her life.

"The next morning," Mrs. O. went on, "I became conscious again of life about me. Encased in plaster and in terrible pain, I saw my daughter's smiling face through a slit in the oxygen tent.

" 'Mother, you are going to be all right. I called Helen Shoemaker and everyone is praying for you,' she said.

" 'Of course I'm going to be all right,' I agreed."

Later Mrs. O. learned that the news of her accident had reached Helen Shoemaker while she was attending a church dinner. Right there prayers were said for Mrs. O. and her sister and their families. Then for days, weeks, and the following months many friends—Catholics, Jews and Protestants—continued prayers in their behalf.

"We know it was the means of pulling us through that

first week when my life hung in the balance," Mrs. O. said. "The thought of dying never entered my mind, although it loomed often in the doctors' consultations."

Six years have passed since her accident. Mrs. O. spent many months in traction in a hospital bed, then more time in a wheelchair. After I saw her she began walking.

"My purpose is not to relate an accident," said Mrs. O., "for many others have suffered similar experiences. I only want to tell everyone *how prayer sustained me and what a mighty force a prayer group can be* when it goes into action. I am convinced that their constant prayer power was the reason for the miracles that took place, one after another, during my convalescence. The doctors were sure I would die that first long week and were certain that complications would set in. In spite of pain I felt an overall sense of harmony that was directly spiritual."

Mrs. O. was quiet for a moment when she finished her story, then looking up at me from her wheelchair she said, "I asked God to use me. I'm so grateful that He did, for my suffering eventually brought spiritual growth to many, including my dear children. My life has been enriched and strengthened by a keen awareness of God's nearness. What more could I desire?"

I met Mrs. O.'s daughter in a prayer group the following morning, and she told me, "This is the prayer group I turned to the night I learned of Mother's accident. As my brother drove my father and me to the town where Mother was hospitalized, I remember saying constantly and *confidently*, 'God, I lift Mother up to Thy healing light.' I knew that God was listening. The nightmare of seeing one I love so dearly in great agony; the shock and the separation from my husband and nine-month-old baby, the horror and grief— all this was made endurable by the state of prayer in which I lived. During the years that followed, my husband and I experienced a deepening of our own religious beliefs. This was a special blessing because ours is a mixed marriage. The

barriers of religious differences diminished considerably when
we were confronted by desperate need. Learning through a
cross is not easy, but for us it has been the means of drawing us together more closely in this most important part
of our lives."

Mrs. O. herself, now able not only to walk but to cook and
keep house, this past year sponsored a study course on "The
Place and Power of the Holy Spirit" which attracted 250
people from all over Pittsburgh. She is one of Helen Shoemaker's team of speakers who go out to speak on prayer
wherever they are asked.

4 * YOUNG COUPLES TRY
PRAYER POWER

One expects to find people past fifty turning to religion, but
to find so many between the ages of twenty and forty disci-
plining their own lives and giving much time to changing
the lives of others was a heartening experience for me. They
believe in the power of prayer to heal the sick, but they also
believe that prayer-centered living is the best kind of preventive medicine.

Doris and Phillip, a young couple, differed somewhat in
their religious training. Doris grew up in the Methodist
church and Phillip in the Episcopal faith. While he was at
college, Phillip wrote a paper stating that Christ's miracles
were frauds and denouncing Christianity in general.

"Oh, I believed there was a God but I could not believe He
was interested in me, or even knew I existed. By this time
Doris and I were married. I divorced myself from the church

and any active faith, feeling I could face the world alone."

"And how about you at this time?" I asked Doris.

"Well, I remained church-minded and felt a growing need more and more," she replied. "Just what kind of a need I did not know." She glanced at her husband. "I made Phillip promise that during our marriage he would go to church with me."

"Did you?" I asked Phillip.

"Yes," he answered and added with all the shrewdness of a lawyer, "I promised to go only twice a month and that included weddings!"

"We went to his church—Calvary Episcopal," Doris said. "Then the Calvary couples began inviting us to the prayer group for our age level [twenties]. Like so many couples we finally said we would go so that they would leave us alone."

Phillip broke in. "I fully expected to find a bunch of crackpots, shouting and laughing. Imagine my surprise to find couples like ourselves, learning the word of God and attempting to solve their daily problems by it. I was impressed but still not ready to buy, confident I could handle any situation alone."

Doris and members of the group told Phillip during discussion that he would run up against a problem that was too tough to solve alone. It came. For a considerable time after he finished law school, he was unable to find the right position. He wanted to practice with a good firm. Doris and the prayer group urged him to talk with Dr. Shoemaker. In sheer desperation and with the attitude that Dr. Shoemaker was his rector, and that he was being paid to help him, Phillip asked Dr. Shoemaker's help, only to have him say he could not help but could give him an introduction to a Friend of his who could. "Dr. Sam," as he is affectionately called by these young people, soon had Phillip on his knees, saying a prayer aloud for the first time in his life.

"I had been with Dr. Sam all Saturday morning but before leaving, I became strangely aware of the power and strength

that is from God. Also I understood how earnestly the prayer
groups were praying for me. It made a great difference."

"Was your problem solved?" I asked.

"No, I still had to find a place to work, but somehow I
knew it would come because I was different."

Doris recalled the special joy that came to her when
Phillip had taken Christ seriously. "Just about this time I
began teaching the Bible as part of my job as a dramatic
teacher, mostly to make extra money until Phillip found his
place. As I taught, the Bible became a great source of help
and strength and comfort, too, during those waiting days."

"The moment Doris and I really began to walk in the way
of a personal commitment," Phillip recalled, "things began
to happen. One Sunday morning after church a man I had
never seen before came up to me and said he had heard I was
a young lawyer looking for a position. Indirectly, he was the
means of leading me to my present job in an excellent law
firm."

"Could this have been just a coincidence?" I asked.

"Well," Phillip answered with a slow grin, "all I can say is
that such coincidences never happened before."

Doris and Phillip had spoken some twenty times in
churches and clubs around Pittsburgh the year I met them
and have been the means through which many young couples
have found a new life through Christ.

"Please do not get the idea that we are on easy street as
far as living this new life goes," said Doris. She went on to
tell me of a terrible argument they had one night just before
they were to go out and speak with Dr. and Mrs. Shoemaker.
They couldn't remember why they had fought.

Phillip said, "I remember I was so darn mad that I went to
bed, refusing to speak, vowing I would at least not be a
hypocrite!"

Doris sat quietly for a while and then went to Phillip and
suggested they pray. Kneeling together by the bed they tried
to pray but all they could do was to ask forgiveness. Suddenly

they were both strongly aware of a presence in the room with them. They turned to each other and both asked the same question: "Didn't you feel God?" Joy flooded their souls and remained with them all evening as they fulfilled their speaking engagement.

"Our prayer group keeps us from thinking only about ourselves, for we continually pray for other couples and all who are in sickness and trouble. We keep healthy and happy because we are no longer filled with negative thoughts. If only every young married couple were fortunate enough to have such a group."

One night I attended the Edgewood Prayer Group, made up of couples between the ages of thirty and forty. It was a wonderful experience sitting in on their earnest Bible study and listening to their prayers of intercession for the ill.

During my stay in Pittsburgh I was advised again and again to talk with Paul O. I gathered he was doing much to inspire new groups and his leadership in a young men's prayer group as well as the Edgewood couples' group was outstanding. Paul, the son of Mrs. O., whose amazing survival after an automobile accident I described earlier, was out of town, but returned just before I was to leave Pittsburgh and graciously consented to an interview. As I talked with him and his wife, Elinor, I learned that he did not consider himself a leader of the prayer group but just one of the members who wanted to give what he had received in new spiritual insight and Christian love.

Paul, an engineer in his late thirties, had organized several prayer groups under Dr. Shoemaker's guidance and was a member of two. The young men's group met weekly during the lunch hour in downtown Pittsburgh, and he and his wife attended the Edgewood couples' group one night each week.

"Please tell me in what way you feel indebted to the prayer groups," I said.

"Our sixteen years of married life have been blessed with

three children and material success," Paul explained. "We were content with our love and life, and with a superficial love for others, until that rainy night our telephone rang and I heard my father's broken voice telling me the news of Mother's accident. Deeply shocked, my father, sister, and I drove through the night to reach her side. Mother has already told you how the power of prayer saved her life. I want you to know what it did for us.

"We attended church but not regularly," Paul said. "We weren't half aware of what the church could offer us. Mother had found something vital. We wanted it, too."

Elinor told me that she and Paul began by joining Calvary Church. After this they helped to organize several prayer groups among the young couples.

"Our home life is so different because of the prayer groups," said Elinor gratefully. "We have developed a prayer life together in our home, with family devotion, grace at the table and reading of the Bible. We are conscious of many failings but we pick up and start again, knowing if we seek God's help He will always answer."

Why have these prayer groups continued to be so influential? Why were they so vital, so interesting? Why did they remain and grow year after year? These were the thoughts that filled my mind after my visit to Pittsburgh.

I came to the conclusion, first, that they were begun jointly by the clergy and laity, each in harmony with the purpose of first changing their own lives through surrender to Christ and then sharing the joys of the new life that was theirs. When a man realizes God's love is at work in his heart, he also knows he must share this love by showing it to others, if he wants to keep that faith alive in his own life. The giving of time in prayer for others is a *must* for every member of a prayer group.

Many times the giving is for people unknown to the group. Take the case of a brilliant young physicist whom we shall call Drew. The parents of two pre-school children, Drew and

Nancy had sacrificed to the limit in order to help Drew complete his requirements for a Ph.D. Although the struggle was hard the young husband and father managed to attain high grades. Then suddenly, when they were in a strange city, far away from any relatives, Drew suffered a breakdown.

When the prayer groups learned of this couple's plight, Drew had been in a psychiatric hospital for three months. Nancy had been forced to put him there because the veterans' hospital did not keep incurables!

Nancy was desperate the afternoon when one of the prayer group visited her for the first time. The shock of being told that her husband was incurable had left her dazed. But Drew was given the maximum number of electric shock treatments and seemingly responded satisfactorily; then, before leaving the hospital, he collapsed while being tested by four of the hospital psychiatrists. He was reported to be in worse condition than when he entered the hospital. As a last resort, insulin shock treatments were begun.

The prayer groups began to keep a prayer vigil for Drew. Meanwhile several of the women kept Nancy's hope alive with phone calls, letters which included tracts on prayer, and short visits during which prayers were said for the young family. The Reverend William Shannon, Dr. Shoemaker's assistant, was an invaluable friend to them and a loyal visitor to the hospital.

Drew began to improve slowly with further treatment. His doctors said, however, that he could not possibly recover for at least two more years, and they could not guarantee a permanent recovery. Meanwhile, Nancy was attending the healing services at Calvary Church and she began taking the books she had read to her husband. He read *The Healing Light*, by Agnes Sanford, and refused to part with it. He read more and more books: *Abundant Living*, by E. Stanley Jones, and many of the sermons of Norman Vincent Peale. He read the books of Samuel Shoemaker.

After eight months at the state hospital, Drew was able to go back to work as a research physicist.

As he looks back upon his nine months as a hopeless schizophrenic, he realizes he could not have been healed at the hospital if he had not had the books on faith to read at that time. He also knows that his collapse came because he had not been taught a faith, and all the knowledge he was acquiring seemed not to provide what he was searching for—something to live by. His wife helped to fill this gap for him through the prayer group. When he was able to surrender to God, release came and with it, healing.

5 * BY THE POWER OF GOD

After serving Calvary Episcopal Church in New York City for almost twenty-seven years, Dr. Shoemaker had a wealth of experience to bring to Calvary Church in East Liberty. But how had his work within his new church branched out from the suburb to the city of Pittsburgh, into business corporations, law firms, steel mills and factories—into what is called the "Pittsburgh Experiment"? This was the first question I put to him as we sat in his study one evening.

"Because I believe that almost everyone feels the need for spiritual power and that the church has the answer to man's needs," Dr. Shoemaker told me. "I was eager to see what could happen if men were persuaded to use Christian principles in their everyday jobs."

In a quiet, unassuming way small groups of men began meeting to discuss how to apply their faith twenty-four hours a day, seven days a week. The Bible was studied and prayers were read by some and said by others. The results were dynamic.

A foreman in a major manufacturing plant was slowly losing his mind from the pressure of his superiors demanding a higher production level and from the grumbling of the workers who felt they were already doing their best. The foreman got ulcers and said his stomach was tied up in knots all the time. Furthermore he was gray with fatigue from lack of sleep. He was asked to attend one of Dr. Shoemaker's Pittsburgh Experiment workshops. The workshop's one theme, "Apply your Christianity," was disappointing. The foreman felt as hopeless as ever after the meeting, but the next time he was called to task by his boss, he made, in desperation, a half-hearted remark that maybe prayer would help. To his utter surprise his superior agreed. These two men began to understand each other's problem and the workers' side of the picture. Through understanding and friendship higher production was reached. The foreman's ulcers healed and he lost his tiredness.

Dr. Shoemaker says that he believes there are times when we need a prayer treatment as definitely as we need a physical massage.

He tells in his book, *By the Power of God*, of a middle-aged man who came to him for counseling. This man was full of fears and an uneasiness he could not understand. He was constantly getting drunk to escape his unnatural feelings.

The man had poured out his problems and felt that his minister understood and cared. When this point had been reached in their relationship, Dr. Shoemaker began a prayer treatment by helping the man to relax—step by step. He asked him, first, to stretch out his feet; to sink back in the armchair where he sat; to rest his arms, then his neck and head against the chair back.

Dr. Shoemaker then prayed release into the man before him. He asked God to heal his nerve ends, muscles, bones, head, heart and to speed up his sluggish circulation. He then prayed for his thoughts, offering his healed mind to God to use according to His will.

The minister then concentrated on the subconscious mind, where this man's real trouble lay. "We visualized our Lord walking down the cellar steps of his mind into these deep, dark, hidden regions where so much of human emotion, good or bad, is generated," said Dr. Shoemaker. "Positive healing is inevitable only when we have peace within ourselves." The minister prayed thoughts of love and forgiveness, belief and creative ideas into the man before him. The time spent in this prayer treatment was approximately fifteen minutes.

When the man opened his eyes, he remarked with some surprise that he felt wonderful. Later his friends began to notice that he was a changed man. Dr. Shoemaker noted, "Spiritual power often manifests itself in the healing of man's mind and body. Jesus is still releasing inner power today as He did when on earth."

Although Dr. Shoemaker is not primarily known as one who carries on a healing ministry, he gratefully acknowledges the fact that healing is often a by-product of the results of concentrated prayer. In the book mentioned above, he tells of a couple who phoned him concerning their small child who had been taken to the hospital, desperately ill, because it could no longer digest its food. The child was sinking rapidly.

On Sunday morning, Dr. Shoemaker hurried to the hospital with the child's father. There he baptized the little boy and made the sign of the Cross on his fevered forehead. Meanwhile the prayer group which the father and mother attended met in a quiet corner of the church to pray for the child's recovery. Improvement began at that moment and today you couldn't find a healthier little boy anywhere. Later, the doctor on the case told Dr. Shoemaker, "It was only by the grace of God that we pulled that kid through."

Dr. Shoemaker told me about Dave G., a young steel-worker who had formed a prayer group which met in the plant at 7:45 A.M., just before the night shift went off and the morning shift began. A few days later I had a chance to interview Dave. His kind of Christianity was contagious, as he told me of all kinds of answers that came from the daily application of faith.

"Dave," I said, "you've got to get me a pass to the plant so I can attend that prayer group."

"Do you know how long it takes to get a pass? About three weeks, if you're lucky!" Dave replied.

I guess I looked disappointed, for he added, "Gee, wish I could but I have already talked with the two men who could get it for you."

"And they said no?"

Dave nodded. Then we both started talking at once. We'd try again. Dave got busy on the phone, but both men still refused. I looked at Dave with his hand still on the phone, head down in thought. Now *he* looked dejected.

So I said, "Think, is there anyone else you could call?"

Dave laughed. "Oh, sure. I could go right to the top boss."

"Well, why not?" I challenged.

Dave found the number and dialed, while I prayed silently.

Dave's brief remarks after he had made his request made it all sound hopeless, but then the tone of his voice changed and his "Yes, sir, thank you sir," was full of victory.

Two days later, at 6:15 A.M., I was met at the entrance gate of the great Homestead Steel works by an official who stayed with me during my entire visit. He first took me to meet several other officials of the public-relations department, who checked my reasons for this visit. When I reached Dave's plant three escorts of official rank who had not previously attended the prayer group decided to go in with me. They told me later that they were highly pleased with what they had witnessed.

I will never forget those fifteen minutes as I looked at the faces of those who lined the walls of a large tool shop. There were approximately forty men, plus two secretaries and myself. About half the men were just coming off the night shift and were in soiled coveralls, their faces and hands smudged with soot. The rest of the men were clean and fresh, about to begin the day shift. One of the men, the leader for that meeting, read a passage from the Bible. Some sentence prayers followed: a prayer of thanksgiving for protection during the night work, an intercessory prayer for one of the men who had suffered an injury, a prayer of petition for understanding and good will as the men worked together. Promptly at the close of the allotted fifteen minutes the prayer group dispersed, some of the men to return home and others to begin another day of work.

This visit to the steel mill was a fitting conclusion to my visit. I came away from Pittsburgh's Calvary Episcopal Church thanking God for a minister and his wife who not only recognized the wide gap between public worship and personal prayer, but who, with unusual insight, were able to lead people to that place of surrender where Christ becomes the worker of miracles in their lives and, through their prayers, the lives of others.

IV

* * *

Healing Through

the Church Clinic

1 * THE DAY I MET
NORMAN VINCENT PEALE

My meeting with the Reverend Doctor Norman Vincent Peale was definitely the result of the power of positive thinking. Eager to delve into the healing ministry of this famous pastor of the Marble Collegiate Church in New York City, I wrote to him asking for an interview.

Two years went by before that goal was reached. My letters were graciously received and promptly answered, but at this time Dr. Peale's book, *The Power of Positive Thinking*, was beginning to soar to unprecedented heights and he was not only being interviewed by reporters from all over the country, but was also much in demand as a speaker. I knew it was impossible for Dr. Peale to fulfill even a small number of the many requests that came to him each day, regardless of his earnest desire to do so. There was nothing to do but to keep trying.

One sultry June morning, the first step toward an interview with Dr. Peale came about unexpectedly. That morning one of our church members, Robert Berry, a young man who was preparing for a career as a medical missionary, was to receive his M.D. degree from Jefferson Medical College in Philadelphia. His wife, Margie, phoned my husband at the church office to say Bob had just managed to secure tickets to his graduation for us, and they hoped we could attend.

A half-hour later, as we drove into the city, my husband informed me that Dr. Peale would be the commencement speaker. I was delighted and my mind flew to the interview I had hoped to have with him. An impossible idea hit me. Maybe I would have a chance to speak to Dr. Peale just long enough to remind him of the long-hoped-for interview.

"Well now!" I laughed. "Who knows? Maybe I'll have a chance to speak to Dr. Peale."

"Oh, sure!" John replied jokingly. "With thousands of people at the Academy of Music, it will be easy!"

"But not impossible if God wants it to happen," I replied. John smiled without comment. I knew this meant he agreed.

Later we found our seats in the top gallery, just as far away as we could possibly be from Dr. Peale, who sat on the Academy stage several levels below us. The situation certainly looked impossible.

Dr. Peale gave a challenging address to the young doctors before him. He told them they were now partners with God to heal man, man who was a spiritual being as well as a physical body. "Your own faith is of great importance," he said. " 'For as the body without the spirit is dead, so faith without works is dead also.' "

The graduation exercises over, we came down many steps to the street below. Inspired by the message we had just heard, I had forgotten for the moment my desire to speak to Dr. Peale. The exit from the top gallery brought us out at the side of the building near the stage door.

Then John spoke quickly. "There he is if you want to speak to him." I looked toward the stage door thinking he meant Bob Berry, for the graduates, still in caps and gowns, were leaving by this exit. Presently I was aware of blocking someone's way. Turning around I came face to face with Dr. Peale! We greeted him, introduced ourselves, and then I told him I'd been trying to get an interview with him for over two years. His genuine interest in us was apparent as he began to apologize for the delayed interview. But not wishing to detain him longer, I laughed and asked, "Shall I keep on trying?"

"Yes, do that. Write to me," he said earnestly. We said good-by and he stepped to the car waiting at the curb. We turned to go but Dr. Peale, with one foot already inside the car, called to me. "Mrs. McKelvey!" He pointed his finger upward, just like a preacher, and grinned broadly as he added, "That's the way to do it; just keep on trying!"

This was the beginning. The interview finally materialized on a beautiful November day, when I met with Dr. Peale in his study at the Marble Collegiate Church.

"I don't suppose you remember the brief meeting we had in Philadelphia at the Academy of Music," I began. He knitted his brow, then his face brightened. "Oh, I see you kept on trying," he recalled. We laughed and then I told him what a thrill it had been for John and me to have that meeting take place.

For the second time I felt this man's genuine interest and insight into the lives of people as he said, "The wonderful part of your faith that day was the fact that you would not have been disappointed if God had not given you your wish, because already in your heart you had accepted whatever the results would be."

That had been my feeling exactly. The complete surrender to God's will, and the belief that His power cannot be limited, had left no room for disappointment. Dr. Peale spoke kindly of some of my articles which he had read and encouraged me to continue writing. He seemed to have a complete understanding as he talked of my threefold purpose in life, as a mother, as a minister's wife, and as one who had an overwhelming desire to serve God through writing. He asked questions about our ministry in Lansdowne and I sensed a longing in him to be active again in parish work. To me it was evident that he missed the closer contacts that come through personal work in one's own church. I asked if this were not so.

"I like nothing better than working with people and I'd be happy if I could spend most of my time in counseling at our church," he replied. "To tell troubled, sick souls about God's healing power is a real privilege."

The more I learned of the life and ministry of Dr. Peale the more I realized that his destiny from birth was being fulfilled in his healing ministry. He was brought into the world by his physician father, who had given up his medical career to devote his life to the Christian ministry. In his home, medicine and religion naturally went hand-in-hand.

Dr. Peale learned as a young minister that God often answers prayers for healing in ways beyond man's comprehension. He told me of his first experience of a supernatural healing, when he was called in the middle of the night to the bedside of the patient of a doctor whom he knew.

"I need your help," said the physician. "I've done all I can. Will you come?"

When young Norman Peale arrived at the home of the patient the doctor explained, "What I want you to do is to fill this sickroom with the healing power of Jesus Christ."

They sat down one on either side of the bed and began to quote Scripture aloud. Dr. Peale recalled how readily just the right verse came to his mind. Then they prayed while the patient tossed restlessly. Through the still hours before morning they gradually came to feel God's presence in the room. The patient grew calm and finally fell into a natural sleep.

"She is out of danger now," announced the doctor. "Let's go home and get some sleep."

"It was nearly five when I started home," Dr. Peale recalled, "but I couldn't think of sleeping and walked the streets, inspired by what I had just witnessed. The patient recovered and lived for many years."

Although Dr. Peale continued to practice and use prayer

power to heal in his own life and ministry, he longed to do something to bring this healing power of Christ back into the churches. The early Christian church had grown and expanded because of it but through the years had lost it. He was convinced, also, that many troubled people were suffering needlessly, having brought on their miserable condition by their unhealthy attitudes. He was greatly strengthened in this belief by a layman of his congregation at the University Methodist Church in Syracuse, New York. This man, Dr. Gordon Hoople, a physician, was convinced that the mind and heart needed treatment as well as the body.

"If it had not been for doctors like my friend Gordon Hoople, and Dr. William Seaman Bambridge and Dr. Clarence W. Leib here in New York," Dr. Peale told me, "I might never have thought of starting a church clinic."

Several interviews followed during the next three years, during which time I came to know Norman Peale and his wife, Ruth, as a consecrated couple who are wholly committed to the tremendous but rewarding service their ministry together has become. If anyone anywhere is engaged in a healing ministry, they are! To feel their love and devotion to Christ their Saviour, their love for each other, and their warm compassion for every afflicted human being, those they meet and those they will never know, is an unforgettable experience.

They meet serenely the mammoth stress and strain resulting from the unexpected fame mushrooming around them only because of their faithful reliance on God's power within them. And they have time to replenish that power daily with God's healing love.

2 * FIFTH AVENUE'S CHURCH CLINIC

Perhaps the last place one might expect to find a church clinic would be on Fifth Avenue in New York City. Just a stone's throw from the tallest building in the world, the Empire State, stands the well-known Marble Collegiate Church. Adjacent to it is the clinic, bordering the church like a good right arm. Here hundreds of people find relief from all kinds of desperate situations, many of which result in physical and mental illnesses.

At the Marble Collegiate Church clinic New Yorkers and people from all over the country find help together. They have learned that in this church they will find those who really care about their problems, and who have time to listen. To find such personal help in this so-called indifferent city is indeed a godsend.

"When I came to Marble Collegiate Church in 1932, the great depression was at its height," Dr. Peale told me, at another meeting with him. "Desperate people were taking their own lives. No middle-aged person could get a job and those who had acquired fortunes now had only worthless stocks. This situation was the same all over the country. Many came to my church study with their problems. I prayed for wisdom, knowing I could not help so many in these desperate times, alone or in my own strength."

The answer to Dr. Peale's prayer came during a Sunday morning church service, as he found himself looking again and again to one of the men in his congregation, Dr. Clarence C. Leib, who was his personal physician. After the service he made an appointment with the doctor.

A few days later in Dr. Leib's office Dr. Peale confessed to his friend, "I need help. I feel certain God has directed me to you. I'm a minister, not a psychiatrist, and I am beginning to sense there is more to the problems of the persons coming to me for help than they themselves realize. Do you know a good psychiatrist who would be willing to give me some insight into these human problems?" he asked.

Not long after this, Dr. Peale found himself in earnest conversation with Dr. Smiley Blanton, a practicing psychoanalyst and Associate Professor of Clinical Psychiatry at Vanderbilt University. He was delighted to find Dr. Blanton in full accord with his own ideas. Often in the past Dr. Blanton had hoped to meet a minister like Dr. Peale, for there were many times he knew his patients needed religion to complete their healing. Here at last was an opportunity to combine the skills of a minister and a doctor in bringing health to those who suffered.

"I would discuss one of the more difficult cases with Dr. Blanton," Dr. Peale explained. "Then he would analyze the man's personality to get to the cause, the cause which the man himself was not aware of. After we discovered the inner conflict, I was able to use the spiritual therapy of faith, prayer and love."

Dr. Peale became more conscious of the fact that his job was to teach people *how* to pray, *how* to have faith and *how* to gain Christ's redeeming love. Dr. Blanton, on the other hand, sent his patients who needed religious training to the minister of the Marble Collegiate Church. Out of this cooperative teamwork eventually grew what was probably the first church clinic in our country.

The joint healing program of Dr. Peale and Dr. Blanton grew by leaps and bounds, far beyond their wildest dream, so that they were compelled to call in more help. Psychiatrists and ministers trained in psychology were added to the staff. Meanwhile Dr. Peale's books on the clinic work and his preaching at the Marble Collegiate Church were making him, much against his own personal wishes, a much sought-after speaker. He realized, however, that God was leading him from the personal counseling of the few to the counseling of masses of people.

Dr. Peale's personal service to the clinic began gradually to decline, except for his executive contribution as president of the board. His preaching and writing began reaching thousands and then finally millions of people.

Furthermore, Dr. Peale's speaking engagements became the answer to the huge financial needs of the quickly expanding clinic. He was therefore content in the fact that so many more were now finding healing in the clinic of his church. Meanwhile the Marble Collegiate Church Clinic became the American Foundation of Religion and Psychiatry. An account of the present work and the stories of many who have received healing there will be told in later chapters.

Concerning his healing ministry, Dr. Peale told me, "I believe only God can heal. I do think there are some persons whom God uses as a channel for his healing power, persons who have the gift of healing. As Paul said, 'For to one is given by the Spirit the word of wisdom; to another the word of knowledge by the same Spirit; to another faith by the same Spirit; to another the gifts of healing by the same Spirit; to another the working of miracles . . .' " (I Corinthians 12: 8-10).

Dr. Peale's interpretation of spiritual healing may be found in chapters eleven and twelve of *The Power of Positive Thinking*. Indeed, healing by faith is found in all his writings because it is a very definite part of his thinking and philosophy of life. His writings on the subject cover all manner of illnesses and are in a language understandable to those not versed in theology or psychology. He gives down-to-earth suggestions on how to practice the right thinking which Jesus taught in His own ministry.

Here are five points Dr. Peale feels are essential when healing is desired:

1. A complete willingness to surrender oneself into the hands of God.

2. A complete release from all error such as sin, in any form, and a desire for soul-cleansing.

3. Belief and faith in the combined therapy of medical science in harmony with the healing power of God.

4. A sincere willingness to accept God's answer whatever it may be and with no irritation or bitterness against His will.

5. A substantial, unquestioning faith that God can heal.

"I merely try to teach the spiritual laws of right thinking according to the Bible," Dr. Peale told me. "I believe that it does bring healing in the body, mind and soul; many write it is so."

The real secret of Dr. Peale's success is not in his label of "positive thinking," for Christian faith has always been an affirmation. His success lies in his method of approach.

"I believe this is the day and generation of the people—the simple people everywhere," he said. "We must not fall into the trap of writing and talking exclusively to and for the favored few who intellectually have had opportunities above those of the masses of the people. It is just as discriminatory to write for the aristocratic intellectuals as it is to favor the aristocrats who are financially favored. We must take the simple, usable, workable, triumphant message of Jesus Christ and put it into a form that will commend it to the people who are not trained in intellectual skills."

At this point Dr. Peale raised a warning finger. "This does not mean that the material must not be intellectually well founded and buttressed at every point. It must be sound in every way and rooted profoundly and deeply in Christian theology and philosophy. But to say it so that people understand it—that is the art."

Just how successful is Dr. Peale's endeavor to teach the simple truths of the Bible in simple language? The answer is that he receives well over five thousand letters every week of his busy life. Among these letters are many reports of physical and mental healing and all of them indicate a new and vital belief in Christ's power at work to change lives when people surrender wholly to His will.

A woman, hopelessly crippled with rheumatoid arthritis for which there is no medical cure, made the long journey from a Western state to attend a Marble Collegiate Church service just to hear Dr. Peale deliver one of his sermons.

"I accidentally turned on the radio to one of your programs," she told Dr. Peale, "just after returning home from a trip to the Mayo Clinic, where they gave me no hope of recovery. Your sermon gave me new faith and I sent for your books and asked that you pray for me."

As she read and prayed and became familiar with the Bible, she discovered that she was full of resentment and worry. She also worked hard on the practical suggestions in Dr. Peale's books. In a few months she could move normally but could only walk a half-block at a time. Eventually her husband had to make a business trip to New York and suggested she go with him to visit Dr. Peale's church. They arrived at the Marble Collegiate Church in time for the evening service. The next day she walked from the Astor Hotel, where she and her husband were staying, to Macy's department store, shopped for several hours, then walked back to the hotel with little discomfort. She was overjoyed and wanted to shout the good news to everyone. "It was so wonderful," she told Dr. Peale, "that I did it again the next day just to prove to myself that I could!"

Nearly all who write to Dr. Peale request some form of his writings—either his books, sermons, "How-to" cards or booklets. I naturally wondered where these letters were answered and how anyone could possibly fulfill all the requests for prayers and literature. When I asked about it Ruth Stafford Peale, who edits all her husband's writings, invited me to visit the Foundation for Christian Living in Pawling, New York.

Dr. Peale smiled proudly at his attractive wife, then, turning to me, he said, "Mrs. Peale is entirely responsible for everything at Pawling. It's her creation!"

3 * DR. PEALE'S HEALING MINISTRY

Anyone writing a letter to Dr. Peale can feel certain it will be read; chances are it may even be read by Dr. Peale himself, but if this is not possible, then either Mrs. Peale, Mrs. Mary Creighton, Dr. Peale's private secretary for many years, or one of the members of the staff at the Foundation for Christian Living, will see it. This organization at Pawling, New York, was Ruth Peale's idea for a systematic and easier way to assist her husband in handling the more than five thousand letters he receives weekly. And a more capable person could not be found, for Dr. Ruth Stafford Peale has earned the right to work side by side with her famous husband; at least Syracuse University thinks so, for in 1956 they conferred upon her the honorary degree of Doctor of Laws.

When I stepped from the train at Pawling, I was met by Mary Rhines Peale, Dr. Peale's gracious stepmother, whose welcome made me feel as if we had known each other for years. We drove through beautiful snow-covered country for about a mile, and arrived at the Foundation simultaneously with the U.S. mail truck. The driver threw off two large sacks bulging with letters. Mary Peale pointed out to me a wing of the building which had recently been added and which was already inadequate to handle the ever-increasing correspondence. En route I had learned from Mary Peale that she was business manager of the Foundation and also a fully ordained minister of the Baptist Church, having served churches for ten years before accepting her present position.

Later as I toured the building I was impressed not so much with the efficiency with which the presses were run, or with the three hundred thousand addressograph plates which daily imprint thousands of envelopes, as with the kind of people who operate the machines in this building. All were church-minded, many teaching in church schools and taking active part in their particular place of worship.

On the upper floor the neat rows of offices were filled with the same high-caliber personnel, from typists to executives. It was difficult to think of these many workers as a business organization—they were this, of course, but so much more. Here was a group of skilled workers dedicated to the cause of Christ. To them the letters they were helping to answer were not mere mail; they were people.

For instance, in one office the main concern of the morning was a letter received from Israel, in which the writer had forgotten to include his address. "It's such a nice letter, too," one of the workers told me, "and how are we going to send the literature he wants?"

One office contained files of letters sent to Dr. Peale in response to his question-and-answer page in *Look* magazine. Two women were engaged in typing the answers Dr. Peale had dictated. All these correspondents' requests for literature are filled free of charge. Another office handles radio mail and in another TV fan letters pile up, many addressed to Mrs. Peale, who shares the program with her husband.

Where do these letters come from? All over the United States, of course, and far and wide throughout the world. I was fascinated to find names filed by country: Arabia, India, Africa (600), Asia, all sections of the British Isles, Jamaica, the British West Indies and all of Europe.

People who write to Dr. Peale include missionaries, college presidents, teachers, doctors, lawyers, housewives, diplomats, congressmen, painters, carpenters, many young people and even children. Letters from teenagers, college students and older youths turn up constantly. Now and then comes a word of encouragement. One high-school boy wrote briefly and to the point on a postcard: "Golly, Mr. Peale, you're swell! Wish we had more pops in the world like you. Keep it up. Tom."

Many crippled and shut-in young people write for Dr. Peale's books and booklets. They want *Thought Conditioners* to help them to adjust to polio and other illnesses that keep them from normal living. Other young people write about all kinds of problems, from dating to overcoming bad health habits. They ask for pamphlets, sometimes a dozen or more, to give to friends who need them.

So many people of all ages ask Dr. Peale to pray for them and their problems that in order to fulfill these requests Dr. and Mrs. Peale long ago established a chapel at the Foundation. Monday of every week is the day of prayer, both at the Foundation and in the *Guideposts* editorial offices in New York City and Carmel, New York.

I learned of this prayer fellowship the year I accepted my first assignment for *Guideposts*. During a briefing conference the executive editor, Len LeSourd, said to me, "We will pray for you, Gertrude, all of us." I began asking questions and learned that the *Guideposts* editors, secretaries, everybody right on down to the beginner clerk, took time to pray together every Monday morning, and on other mornings as well if there was some special need or occasion for thanksgiving.

The Pawling chapel I visited was small, accommodating only six at a time (a new and larger chapel has now replaced it), but it was exquisite. Mary Peale and I sat together in this chapel. In her hands were over a hundred prayer cards. On each card was typed the name and prayer request taken from a letter written to Dr. Peale. As members of the staff gather for the prayer service each one meditates on the person and problem listed on one of these cards. On leaving the chapel he places the card on the altar.

"How long is the prayer time allotted to each employee?" I asked Mary.

"There is no time limit or condition of any sort," she replied. "One may stay as long or as short a time as is desired, praying for one or several persons."

What were the prayer requests on the cards in Mary's hand? She pointed some of them out to me. A woman hating her sister to the extent that she was chronically ill said, "Pray that I can overcome hate with love and grow healthy and happy once more."

A teen-age girl wanted prayer for her mother afflicted with cancer. A college student needed help in learning how to pray for healing and the right attitude regarding his polio condition. So many requests came from cancer patients, people with heart trouble, arthritis, mental illness. The list was long.

But many letters to Dr. Peale requested prayers of thanksgiving for healings received: "Thank you for your help, Dr. Peale, and please join me in thanking God for His healing power."

Mary said, "It is a real joy to be able to remove the name of a person who has recovered from our prayer list, after we have offered our thanksgiving, too." An example, she said, was a woman whose husband had written some weeks ago, asking prayers for his wife who suffered from an acute asthmatic condition, making it impossible for her to sleep lying down. Medical help failed to bring relief.

One evening the husband read aloud to his wife from the booklet, *Spirit Lifters*, in which Dr. Peale had written that anyone could experience Christ's healing power. The couple decided to try it. The husband read the Bible to his wife and then he prayed. The wife wanted to pray and did the best she could between gasping breaths, saying, "I believe, Lord—heal me." They sat quietly, thanking God for their blessings, and gradually the wife's breathing grew easier, and then became normal. They felt the presence of Christ there with them. That night for the first time in over a year she was able to sleep lying down. She has had no trouble since.

Mary Peale and I left the chapel and she directed me to the large study at the top of the building where I found Dr. and Mrs. Peale, answering letters. They had a chair waiting for me, beside the huge desk. Letters lay in neat piles, with many answers already dictated and ready for the typists. I sat spellbound as they told me of the contents of some of these letters.

A great many alcoholics, I learned, found help from Dr. Peale's sermons, speeches and writings. A young GI wrote, "Eight months ago I was in the hospital here at the base, down and out from drinking, and this was my third hospital trip. But this time someone placed one of your books in my hand and what I read sent me to AA. I am very happy to say that I haven't had a drink since which is over eight months. Following God's way has brought me the peace and health your books and sermons have told me I could have."

Another member of Alcoholics Anonymous wrote telling Dr. Peale that he never had any religion because he had not been taught to believe when a child. "Now that I want a faith, I find it so difficult to understand. One of my AA pals put your book in my hands and for the first time I'm beginning to understand the Bible. Would like to receive your sermons. I'm sure I am on the way to real faith in God. Thank you."

"Now this wonderful woman has a real sense of humor," said Dr. Peale, as he told me of a registered nurse, the wife of an alcoholic, who wrote that his book, *The Power of Positive Thinking,* helped her to understand and help her husband, who is now on his way to a strong recovery with help from AA. He has been working every day for two years and in his spare time speaks to other alcoholics in prisons and state hospitals. They have six children, the last twin boys

(born after the husband's recovery) who are joyfully referred
to as their AA babies!

Later, at lunch with Dr. and Mrs. Peale, we talked of the
need we all had for constant awareness of our Lord in our
daily living. We talked of Jesus' ministry. At one point Dr.
Peale said, "Gertrude, surrender to Christ must be the message of your book. Only when a person gives himself to Jesus,
with nothing held back, can God give us the abundant life
he promised. Then if we do all we can to bring about our
healing we should expect God to do the impossible."

I looked at Ruth, as she quietly nodded in affirmation. She
is so different from her husband, who radiates his enthusiasm
with the strong voice of conviction, often accompanied by
gestures. Ruth Stafford Peale, more reserved, impressed me
as one whose sympathetic nature brings quiet comfort to
her husband in his busy career. Both are humble people, aware
of the fact that all they have and anything they are able to
achieve for others comes directly through them from God.
In humbly serving their Lord, they find their greatest satisfaction for living.

After lunch, back at the Foundation, Ruth Peale, with her
hands full of letters, explained further how people found
God's healing power through her husband's ministry. She
told me of a man from Lancaster, England, who wrote, "I
began reading your book, A *Guide to Confident Living*, from
the *Daily News*, and want you to know it has completely
changed my life." He began practicing Christian principles in
his business dealings and climbed from eighty-first place to
fourth place in his firm.

One day, however, his six-year-old son came down with
all the symptoms of polio—high temperature and a very stiff
neck and legs. He could not move his head forward. The
doctor called twice that day and took a grave view of the
child's condition. The father went to his room, alone, and
reread Dr. Peale's chapter on healing. He prayed, putting his
little son entirely in God's hands.

"I cannot honestly say whether my son had polio," he wrote, "but at any rate, I know that his condition began to improve at once and by the following day he was well. The doctor now thinks it was only flu but said it certainly looked like polio!"

A woman from Canada told of her husband's mental illness, which resulted in a nervous breakdown necessitating a six weeks' stay in a mental institution. In addition he suffered from a duodenal ulcer for five years and had also had a coronary attack. All this was caused from worry over reverses in his business. His wife, distraught, bought for his fifty-seventh birthday one of Dr. Peale's books.

One night, desperately realizing that he was slipping back mentally, he finally picked up *The Power of Positive Thinking* and began to read. "I prayed, oh so hard, while he read," wrote his wife. "God answered my prayers, for he finished the first chapter, bowed his head, and gave himself and his illness to God. Then I began quietly to read to him from *Thought Conditioners*. We had a wonderful evening as we both prayed and talked about how merciful God is to those who trust Him."

The husband then went to bed and slept soundly for the first time in years, got up the next morning renewed and happy. As his wife put it, "He went to work this morning with an almost forgotten spring in his step and with *Thought Conditioners* in his pocket!"

Another man wrote: "My business is gone, my funds exhausted and I am paralyzed from head to toe with only a small amount of mobility left. A friend brought me *Spirit Lifters*. Now I am learning to walk again, and my faith is restored. I know I will recover. Please send me two more copies for some friends."

Another claimed:

When I was told I had cancer I secretly prayed that I would die during the operation, but I had your *Thought Conditioners* with me, and before the operation I prayed that God's will be done. When I woke from the operation I knew God had something more for me to do. I recovered speedily, and beyond all my surgeon's expectations! Your beautiful explanation of Isaiah 40:31 pulled me through. "But they that wait upon the Lord shall renew their strength; they shall mount up with wings as eagles; they shall run, and not be weary; and they shall walk and not faint." It is a miracle!

"This woman," said Ruth Peale, taking up another letter, "lives alone and supports herself. She had difficulty with her bronchial tubes due to a frost-bitten condition a few years ago. She writes as follows: 'Catching a cold meant a trying time for me. But I decided to put myself completely in God's hands as you suggested. I asked Jesus to put his healing hands on my chest and then I fell asleep. I dreamed that someone came into my room, put their hands on my chest and then gently turned me over and did the same thing to my back. I woke the next morning with no sign of a cold.' "

This woman went on to say that although she has many faults, she is trying to overcome them and bring cheer to others where she works. "Maybe this is one way to spread the work Jesus began on earth. I know I can't talk religion for they would shy away, but pray for me that I can live it every day."

Ruth Peale then had to leave me for another appointment. We parted in Mary Peale's office. Mary had a few more letters to show me which illustrated the different ways Norman Vincent Peale reaches people.

A very tired and concerned young mother of three pre-school children, one a badly burned six-month-old baby, was so depressed that she felt God just didn't care about her prayers. The times were hard and she had no help with the cleaning, washing, ironing and cooking for her husband and the children. The baby had suffered a third-degree burn on his forehead and was nearly blind from the swelling. She turned the dial slowly on her broken-down radio, hoping to find music to raise her spirits. Instead she heard Dr. Peale in his Sunday-morning radio broadcast.

"I don't remember what you said," the young woman wrote Dr. Peale later, "I only know that God was in your heart and I knew my baby would get well." When the sermon had ended, the young mother heard the congregation singing a hymn. As the music warmed her heart she prayed that God would restore her baby. Now she knew God was hearing her prayers and that He loved her.

Less than an hour later the baby began to eat and the mother reported that at the end of three weeks the child had completely recovered.

"The day I saw you as a guest on the Arlene Francis Home Show, you were introduced as the man whose book had changed the lives of thousands of people," wrote a woman from the West coast to Dr. Peale. This woman told herself that she certainly needed changing, for she was miserable. She believed all church people were hypocrites and that all religion was a plain racket. She was chronically ill, having undergone several operations.

One day her doctor told her he could do no more for her; that she would have to change her attitude and face up to life. At first she was enraged at her doctor's frankness but her anger subsided and she went out to buy some books on psychology.

> That's when I found your book *The Power of Positive Thinking*. If I had known it was a religious book, I never would have bought it! I read it through to the end and then started on the Bible and tried to pray as you suggested. It helped me eventually to see myself as I was, hateful, selfish and critical of others. Now I've learned to look to God for faith and at my sins instead of those of others. It is amazing how much I can find to do for other people as well as for my family. Pray for me sometimes. Thank you and God bless you.

There are many more letters that witness to all kinds of healing of body, mind and soul which might be related here. However, I wish to quote this final one in its entirety because it so well exemplifies the gift that is Norman Vincent Peale's in transmitting great Christian truths in simple, practical, workable language into the lives of people everywhere who believe in God's healing power.

Dear Dr. Peale: I wish to take this time to thank you for the immeasurable help I have received from your books and sermons. Time and again they have set me straight in my thinking and inspired me to renewed faith in the goodness of God and people.

In May I had occasion to reread several of your sermons and sections of your books on the subject of thankfulness to God for help received and ways of expressing it. In so doing I became convinced that I must make a renewed and complete dedication of my life to God. There have been two sins of long standing which I never succeeded in overcoming for long. You recommended confiding in one's pastor and at last with the help of his prayers, I have succeeded.

Just after this experience, I became aware of a serious loss of vision in one eye. On examination it was discovered that the retina was almost completely detached. God was good in guiding me to an excellent surgeon and he operated on a Friday. Sunday when the doctor dressed it he checked it for vision. I could see straight ahead which I couldn't do before, but on Tuesday he checked again and found my vision to be slipping.

I tried all day to believe in the promises of answered prayer and when night and lights out came, I had a real battle with my fears and doubts. Then I remembered your discussion in the chapter "How Power and Efficiency Can Be Yours" in A *Guide to Confident Living* and the verse from St. Mark 11:23-24. Then I realized if I were really believing, I would have a deep sense of trust rather than a battle of fear.

A great peace came over me and I slept as I had not been able to since the discovery of my eye trouble. The next day the medication proved irritating and was changed. The next examination showed a marked improvement and my vision is continually better. Thank you again.

As Mary Peale drove me to the railroad station, I tried to thank her as I had tried to express my gratitude to Dr. and Mrs. Peale.

"It's been a wonderful day," I said. "I appreciate all the time and effort you have given me. And you, too, are doing a fine work."

Mary smiled. "Ruth and Norman are the inspiration and brains behind all we do," she said, quietly. "The rest of us just keep the wheels running."

This was the first time I had ever thought of a healing ministry on wheels. But on wheels it was, the wheels of the mail trucks and trains and planes. And at that very moment, the wheels were turning, carrying copies of Dr. Norman Vincent Peale's sermons to approximately three hundred thousand people all over the face of the globe! All this was made possible by a minister's wife, whose missionary zeal to spread the healing gospel to the uttermost parts of the earth is succeeding.

Ruth Stafford Peale is always ready to take one more leap on faith, and why not? As she succinctly remarked, "The Foundation has been running on faith from the beginning; I see no reason to lower our sights now."

4 ∗ A *GUIDEPOSTS* HEALING

A Christian is expected to be a radiantly happy person, no matter what! But let's face it: all of us are human and subject to human reactions all the time and these sometimes war on radiance. What, for instance would be your initial reaction if your doctor told you that he had found you had a malignant melanoma, or cancer, of the ear? You just might be able to muster up a positive thought, hoping as your

100] FINDING GOD'S HEALING POWER

doctor explained your disease that he might say it wasn't so bad, perhaps even curable, as many types of cancer are today. But suppose he says, "It's a particularly vicious kind of cancer, especially if it gets into the blood stream. In all probability you are going to die."

Elizabeth and John Sherrill, in their early thirties, told me they were too shocked to register any emotion when the doctor gave them this report on John's condition. We three were lunching in a quiet New York restaurant not far from *Guideposts'* editorial offices, where John is a senior editor.

"We learned that shock is a defense mechanism for the body, which enables one to remain perfectly calm under desperate circumstances," John told me. "Without an operation the statistics were one chance in nine of my being alive at the end of the year (it was then September 20, 1957). Even with an operation I had only one chance in three."

The doctor advised John to get at least two other opinions. Elizabeth went back to their suburban home to the children, aged one, four and seven. John, with his X-rays under his arm, started making the rounds of the hospitals.

"I walked to the first hospital whistling and humming," John recalled. "It was a beautiful fall day with every tree a mass of glorious color. Before I reached home several hours later, I even joked with some workmen repairing the road. I do not remember what we laughed about—but I was able to laugh because my body defenses, which had set up a wall against the bad news, had not yet broken down. This wasn't being brave, you know. It was the reaction to the shock, over which I had no control."

Late that afternoon John arrived home with reports from two hospitals: malignant melanoma. Immediate surgery was advised. The third report would reach them Monday. Without a word they went up to John's study and, at last, began to cry without embarrassment. With the shock defense gone they now experienced the torture of fear, which began to harry them constantly. For the children's sake, they tried to keep their minds on other things, but fear hung over them like a dagger. Nevertheless, they managed to take the necessary steps, and spent hours going over insurance, a will and finances. With these matters out of the way, John turned again to his work.

Then something wonderful began to happen. On John's desk lay an unfinished manuscript he had been writing for *Guideposts*, on prayer. It was titled: "Why Do Men Pray?" John had concluded that one reason was to ask for God's divine help in man's hour of helplessness. Elizabeth and John had asked for that help as best they could, but now they were to see that prayer answered. The phone began to ring and continued ringing as friends heard the news. Letters arrived from friends, and even from friends of friends whom the Sherrills had never met.

"The first phone call came from Dr. Peale," John told me. "He had just returned from a speaking engagement. He talked a long time, with a love and understanding that overwhelmed me. The first small ray of hope began slowly to penetrate the stranglehold that fear had upon me. He talked with Elizabeth, too."

After the call, their minds were ringing with the verses from the Bible which Dr. Peale had quoted with stirring conviction. Christ's words to his disciples during the Last Supper now had a strong new power. "In the world ye shall have tribulation: but be of good cheer; I have overcome the world."

The next morning Dr. Peale offered a prayer in their behalf during the Sunday-morning service at Marble Collegiate Church. Prayer power seemed to rise around John and Elizabeth, like a protective cloak.

I'll never forget John's thoughtful smile as he told me of the tenderness with which he regarded the concern of *Guideposts*' assistant art director, Sal Lazzarotti, who almost drove off the road on his way home as he prayed for John. He kept repeating, "I haven't been saying the Rosary regularly, God, but from now on it's going to be different!"

Another friend had prayers said at her synagogue. A night-club singer who hadn't been in church for years slipped into a Catholic chapel to light candles for the Sherrills. Elizabeth and John had known their health-insurance agent as a fun-loving, poker-playing businessman. But in a letter explaining insurance coverage, he wrote, "Don't forget to pray. Remember all things are possible with prayer."

A peace finally settled down over John and Elizabeth during those few days before the report came from the third hospital. It was the same as those received from the other two: malignant melanoma. Immediate surgery! John was admitted to the hospital on Thursday for an operation Friday.

Now as we three talked about the deep inner aspects of prayer, John explained that this calming peace remained with him, the result of prayer. All through the night before the operation he realized he had lost every vestige of the fear that had tormented him.

"How did you pray, John?" I asked.

Elizabeth answered for him. "John prayed constantly for others, a habit he has had ever since I've known him," she said. "He has always had a quiet trust in God's love and tries constantly to surrender all of his life to Him."

After the operation the surgeon told John, "Your report is the best possible one I could bring you. There is no evidence of residual melanoma."

"When I learned that I had cancer," John concluded, "fear became a monster which had the power to destroy just as surely as did the melanoma. I experienced the power of prayer to overcome the worst disease of all—fear."

John Sherrill and his wife could have dwelt on some negative thoughts: Did the surgeon remove all the cancer? Will it return? Am I really cured? But they had learned always to rely on positive affirmations such as this one in II Timothy 1:7: "For God hath not given us the spirit of *fear*; but of power, and of love, and of a sound mind."

And what's more, they know it works!

Every true healing experience brings a wholeness. The many extra rewards to answered prayer are unlimited. John and Elizabeth Sherrill will tell you that John's healing brought to each of them a deeper awareness of God's willingness to give divine power to those who trust in Him. It is a truth which is beautifully expressed by Jeremiah to the weary souls in exile: "Then shall ye call upon me, and ye shall go and pray unto me and I will harken unto you. And ye shall seek me, and find me, when you shall search for me with all your heart. And I will be found of you, saith the Lord" (Jeremiah 29:12-14).

5 * PSYCHOLOGY GOES
TO CHURCH

The American Foundation of Religion and Psychiatry (formerly the Marble Collegiate Church Clinic) maintains 32 trained persons who listen day by day, year in and year out, to hundreds of persons who are sick in mind, body and soul. The skilled teamwork of 14 minister-psychologists, eight physician-psychiatrists, four psychologists and one psychiatric social worker bring many to the church clinic in search of healing for themselves or for someone in whom they are deeply interested.

Some feel they will receive more understanding sympathy in a church clinic than in a psychiatrist's office. Also there are those who cannot afford to pay the average basic fee of twenty-five dollars for psychiatric consultation. Others have spent a small fortune going the rounds from one doctor's office to another only to be told, and rightly so, that there is nothing physically wrong. Not satisfied and still miserable, many become the easy prey of charlatans who promise to restore health quickly. For these and many other reasons they come at last to the church clinic.

It would require a book in itself to tell of the hundreds who have received healing since the first church clinic began at Marble Collegiate Church in 1937 and of the progress being made through the teamwork of the 32 present professional counselors. However, the layman can begin to understand how religion and psychology bring health to many desperate souls through an account of the counseling of the minister-psychologist, the Reverend Clinton J. Kew.

In 1949 Dr. Peale invited Clinton Kew to join the staff of the Marble Collegiate Church Clinic. The Reverend Kew came well equipped, having had many years' experience in large and small parishes as well as holding a university professorship in the fields of psychology and philosophy. With a degree from the University of Vermont, plus graduate study at Berkeley Divinity School and the Virginia Theological Seminary, he also received the degree of Bachelor of Sacred Theology from Harvard University.

When he was a sophomore in college his class was taken on an observation trip to a mental hospital. This made such an impression upon him that he became vitally interested in the field of human behavior. Gradually his interests turned toward religion, and later, toward psychology. His experience at the hospital stirred his love and compassion for people. "The place gripped me," the Reverend Kew told me. "Not only because it was so pathetic and seemingly hopeless, but because after that experience I could never escape one thought: 'Most of this was unnecessary!' "

He decided that he must learn how to help those who could not help themselves and to give courage to the many who were distressed and without hope. He became convinced that psychology needed religion and that religion needed psychology.

Before joining the staff at the Marble Collegiate Church Clinton Kew gained wide experience through teaching psychology, doing pastoral counseling and parish work all during the war years and, for a short time, serving as a part-time chaplain at the famous Bellevue Hospital. He obtained his background in the ministry while serving as rector in several Episcopal churches.

When he joined the staff of the Marble Collegiate Church clinic, he was asked to conduct healing services in the Church of the Heavenly Rest and later in the Church of the Ascension, both on Fifth Avenue in New York City. At present he is conducting a weekly healing service in the Marble Collegiate Church.

During one of my interviews with the Reverend Kew, his secretary came into the office to ask him if he would take a phone call which she thought was important. (He is seldom interrupted when in conference.) "I thought you would want to take this call," she said.

For the next few minutes Clinton Kew listened to a highly excited voice. I could not help hearing some of the conversation. With reassuring comments, he quietly answered this obviously disturbed person.

"I am in conference now," he said, "but I can say by all means stick to your religion. Yes, I will be glad to see you." He switched the call back to his secretary so an appointment could be made.

"I gather you heard that?" he said.

"Some, but not all," I admitted.

"That was a woman who has been going to a psychiatrist who told her to forget her religion because it was confusing her badly. She feels threatened; she feels stripped of her defenses. If her religion is neurotic, then it is better to remove the motivation for it; to remove the anger and fear associated with it. But if her religion is not neurotically inclined, then her faith would be a determining factor toward her recovery."

"Does this happen often?" I asked.

"Many persons coming to our church clinic," he replied,

"have an added problem because they have been told to forget their religion. One doctor makes a particular point of disregarding and attacking religion. Many people resent this doctor's attitude and come to us from his office. On the other hand, we send many patients to psychiatrists all over the city, one important reason being that we realize some people have certain emotional blocks which must be removed before a patient can come close to God."

I learned from the Reverend Kew that the church atmosphere quickly erases the conception many persons have of psychotherapy—that it is only for the neurotic and the insane. At the American Foundation clinic many normal individuals have found a fuller and more interesting life as a result of the therapy they have received.

"Physical ailments have disappeared in many cases," Clinton Kew told me. "Many tell me that all they needed was the healing service. Some find confidence restored in the quiet of the church; others state that the laying-on-of-hands gives a spiritual side to their analysis. And some, like Virginia, are healed physically in a quiet way. Her story is also an example of what a hindrance 'hate' can be in a recovery.

"Virginia came to the healing service every week for six months, and each time she came to the altar to receive the laying-on-of-hands for prayers for her particular disability. After every service she would quietly greet me at the door, express her thanks for the help received, and go out without another word. She was thin and I judged not in good physical condition, but as time passed she began to look stronger, more alert and cheerful. One day she unexpectedly asked, 'Do you like to hear good things?' "

"I most certainly do," the Reverend Kew answered.

"Then I want to tell you that my healing has been completed here in your church," she said.

"I often wondered about you," he admitted.

She made an appointment with him to come to the clinic

and tell him of her experience. The Reverend Kew asked her if she would like to share her story with me as I was writing a book about these experiences. She readily consented and we met together in one of the small consulting rooms.

I learned that Virginia had endured almost every kind of pain, physical, mental and spiritual. By the time she was twenty-three, she had been through protracted spells of excruciating pain, the misery of deep depressions, fever, and an intense hatred for everyone. "I had so many operations, I lost count," she told me.

She went to various hospitals for one treatment or another. One doctor would tell her that this therapy would save her life, another that the next operation might heal her. She spent long, lonely periods in the Adirondacks taking rest treatments, but to no avail.

"Finally I ended up in Bellevue Hospital minus a few ribs," she told me. "It is hard to tell you all the feelings I experienced through those dreadfully long years. There were times when I wanted to take my life. And there was a period when I fought the thought of having operations, afraid that when I took the anesthesia I would never wake up. While awake I would fight for every breath."

"Did your religious faith give you help during those years?" I asked.

"No," Virginia answered without a moment's hesitation. "I didn't have much religion, for my parents sent me to church school but never went with me. I learned early to resent this because I wanted to stay home on cold and rainy Sundays and look at the funny papers, too, as my parents did. One day when I was in dreadful pain at the hospital, the minister called to see me."

"Did you feel that his visit was helpful?" I asked.

"No," came her emphatic reply. "He made me talk when I was in pain and I finally told him I did not believe in God because God didn't know I was around. I guess I shocked him for he could only reply, 'My child, what's happened to your faith?'

"My thoughts were bitter and I wondered if he would have his faith if he could feel the pain I had just then."

One day, as Virginia lay trying to endure the ever-present pain, she opened her eyes to look up at the smiling face of a nurse's aide. In a quiet voice she told Virginia, "I have times of pain too, but when it comes I pray and then I have peace of mind." After that the aide came every day for a short visit with Virginia, who found herself looking forward to seeing Lovely Light, for that was the name given her by Father Divine, the leader of a sect to which Lovely Light had pledged her loyalty. "Even though I could never accept the kind of religion that gave Lovely Light her great faith," Virginia told me, "I longed to be able to believe in something as earnestly as she did."

About this time, one of Virginia's few visitors left a copy of C. S. Lewis's book, *Mere Christianity*, on her bed table. She tried to read it on her better days. It impressed her, in part, but much of it baffled her because of her spiritual immaturity.

One of the chaplains at Bellevue also visited her. She was cold at first, not welcoming his calls, for she was filled with resentment and she was afraid he would preach to her as had the other minister.

Virginia's face became radiant as she told me about the chaplain. "He was different from the picture I had in my mind of a minister. The first time I warmed up to him a little he asked me if he might just call on me as a friend and not as a chaplain. He also promised he would not discuss religion unless I asked him to do so."

The chaplain became Virginia's best friend in the days that followed and soon she was asking him to explain some of the book, *Mere Christianity*, which had so baffled her.

She was scheduled to undergo a serious operation for the removal of a lung. Her weakened condition left the doctors doubtful of her recovery, yet they felt the operation was imperative.

"The chaplain now came every day to see me and his prayers brought comfort while he was with me. But after he left I would be afraid again. Just before the operation he told me he would be there with me until it was over. I didn't feel so alone then."

The chaplain kept his promise. During Virginia's operation he sat in a corner of the operating room, in meditation, reading his Bible from time to time as his lips moved in prayer. Once, during the last part of the six-hour operation, Virginia stopped breathing. The surgeon gave the chaplain a quick glance across the room. In a few moments her breathing began again and held for the rest of the operation.

"When I came out of the anesthetic hours later there stood my chaplain smiling down at me," Virginia said. "For days I was too weak to talk but he would come quietly to my bed every day to say a short prayer. Sometimes when I was so ill that the sound of a voice was torture, he would sit by my bed without a word, but I knew that he would pray silently before he left. At other times, when I was stronger, he would say a short prayer standing by my bed, then smile and leave. I'm sure it was the chaplain's faith that pulled me through."

As she grew stronger and learned of the vigil of prayer the chaplain had kept for her in the operating room, she began asking all kinds of questions about religion. She began to feel love for more people. Religion began to make sense to her as the chaplain answered her many questions. One day as they talked about the meaning of surrender to God, Virginia comprehended God's love for her, for the first time in her life.

"After the chaplain left my room, I lay thinking of our discussion," she recalled. "I now wanted to believe, to know God as the chaplain did, as my best Friend. Then I recalled how on one occasion I had endured excruciating pain, when it was necessary to pump air into my lungs." (This painful treatment required the aid of three nurses while an intern injected a long needle into her side.) "Reliving this awful experience, I suddenly visualized Jesus on the Cross, suffering for me because He loved me. The chaplain said that Christ had suffered gladly, willingly!"

Now Virginia understood the word compassion. She knew why the chaplain had given her so much of his time, why Lovely Light had been so kind. Her heart filled with love for both of them. She grew steadily stronger and was released from the hospital even though she was still far from a complete recovery. Doctors said another operation should be performed but they could only promise her a 20-per-cent chance for a complete cure.

She came home with a drainage tube in her side. Later, when the tube was removed, the opening would not heal.

"I felt confident that God would not let me down," Virginia said earnestly. "I felt if the hospital could give me a twenty-per-cent chance with another operation, God *would* and *could* give me a much better chance. I prayed for guidance.

"Then, while listening to the radio one day, I heard about the healing service. You know the rest. I came every week and gradually the opening in my side healed. At the end of six months I was strong and well."

Virginia also came regularly for interviews, in addition to attending the church services. Through this weekly counseling, she was able to grow emotionally and receive the security which filled the great void in her spirit. She received both mental and emotional support. She was able to mature and ultimately, through the combination of the worship services and psychology, she became free of her hostility, fear, anxiety and illness. "I am come that they might have life, and that they might have it more abundantly" (John 10:10).

Four years have passed since her healing and she is in good health and manages a sizable business which she thoroughly enjoys.

On another visit to the clinic I asked Clinton Kew, "Do unbelievers or those not interested in religion come to a church clinic?"

"Yes, they do," he replied. "After going the rounds and finding themselves still desperate, many come to church as a last resort."

I talked with Diana, who was one of those who came to the church clinic for just such a reason. "I hadn't been inside a church for ten years," she told me.

Diana spoke freely and I soon learned that she had traveled extensively and knew people all over the world. Whirling through life at top speed, she found it empty. She was a hollow shell. At the age of forty she was fast becoming an alcoholic. She became thin, nervous, full of anxiety and resentment. She came from a good family and her mother, a faithful churchwoman, was deeply concerned about her. One Sunday her mother suggested she attend the Marble Collegiate Church.

"I laughed, a bit hysterically I'll admit," Diana explained. "I made it plain to Mother I didn't need the church. That was for people who had no backbone, were blind and needed a handle to hang on to."

But Diana did eventually go to the Marble Collegiate Church with her mother just to please her. Dr. Peale preached on a text from Psalm 55:22, "Cast thy burden upon the Lord, and He shall sustain thee."

"That kind of weak-kneed philosophy I'll never buy," Diana thought as she sat in the pew. Then, for something to do while the sermon continued, she began reading the announcements on the back page of the church calendar in her hand. She became deeply interested in reading about the Marble Collegiate Church Clinic and in a question: "Do you need help in solving a problem which has become too big for you to handle alone?"

As all the misery of her present condition flooded her mind

and heart again, she inwardly admitted, "I surely do." Deep within, she knew she couldn't handle her problems alone—she couldn't even trust God.

Then she discovered that, although this church had a clinic, it was staffed by psychiatrists and ministers. The thought of going to a minister for help was deplorable to her. She was sure she did not need a psychiatrist but she decided she could respect a psychologist and seek his help.

The next day Diana went to the Church Clinic and asked to see a psychologist; she insisted she would not talk to a minister. She was assigned to Clifton E. Kew, the twin brother of the Reverend Clinton Kew. After three months of weekly sessions she began to understand why she was filled with anxiety and resentment. The psychologist helped her to see that she was a perfectionist who had no patience with those around her—people who, to her way of thinking, did everything only half right. She trusted others only half-heartedly. She realized that she couldn't trust herself; she had no faith in herself.

At the end of the three months, it was suggested that she see a clergyman. This time she did not object, for she was beginning to sense that she needed a power beyond herself. She went to the Reverend Clinton Kew and he gradually helped her to find strength in prayer and comfort in private and group worship. From daily reading of the Bible, she learned more of the true meaning of love.

Diana faithfully attended the healing services at the church. Then one day, while kneeling at the altar rail to receive the laying-on-of-hands and prayers for healing, she knew she would never take a drink again. Complete healing soon followed. She regained her lost weight and her headaches and depression disappeared. Today Diana is very much alive with the joy of living a life of surrender to God. She is a radiant personality with a purpose in life. Always an avid reader, she now finds the Bible her most inspiring book.

"I still have so much to learn," Diana told me, "but God

is revealed to me in so many different ways. I'm beginning to learn how to seek His guidance in everything I do. I am free to express my gratitude to Him now. I shall never be able to praise God enough for the peace and joy I have found."

I attended the healing service with Diana that day at noon. As we knelt at the altar together, I too was thankful to God for revealing Himself to this lovely woman, who not so long ago was a lost and wretched soul.

Diana, unlike Virginia, refused to come to the church at first, but went in through the back door of the clinic; there a trained psychologist and a minister, skilled in pastoral counseling, were able to help her open the front door of the church and "Enter into His gates with thanksgiving."

6 * THE HIGH PRICE
OF HEALING

All who seek help at the American Foundation of Religion and Psychiatry clinic learn that the surrender of "self" to Christ without reservations is the only requirement for abundant life now and eternal life after death. There are no compromises involved in finding "the Way, the Truth and the Life." Unfortunately there are always those who, though given every opportunity, miss the point entirely in their quest for fulfillment in life.

One man, who had been under psychiatric treatment in several other places, came to the Reverend Kew, saying: "I would like to give religion a whirl for an hour or two. That just may be the answer." He wanted religion to accomplish in two hours what one of his psychiatrists had failed to do in four years. Several years later this man was taken by force to an institution for the insane.

This is an extreme case, of course, but there are many normal persons who go just so far in their surrender of self and no farther. When the price of abundant life comes too high, they begin making excuses: "If I only had some time to read religious books." "I simply can't go to church because I work six days a week and have to do my washing and cleaning on Sunday." "I don't need communion and confession." "I don't like the minister's sermons and never get anything out of them." "Why must I worship God in church when I can do it out of doors?"

Regarding psychotherapy, attitudes like these are prevalent: "Well, I've tried religion, now I'll see what the psychologists can do." "He didn't say a thing to help me." "I can't afford two sessions a week (even at clinical rates), so I guess it will be cheaper to stay sick." Some who do come regularly for treatment begin to rid themselves of wrong attitudes that keep them from God, but sometimes they will not make the final step, which is often the most difficult. Going through the motions is not enough. Dr. Peale, founder of the clinic, repeatedly expresses this thought: "For the impossible to happen man must first do the possible."

As Clinton Kew puts it in the book *You Can Be Healed*, "The grasp of remedy by the intellect doesn't mean that the *inner forces of the soul have been touched*. What we need in the world today is less intellectualism and more emotion in our lives, more spiritual and psychological thinking to go hand in hand with the mental processes. The love Christ speaks of is not mechanical, not of the intellect alone, but of the heart as well."

June Andover, as we will call her, a twenty-three-year-old girl who graduated from college *cum laude* and has a Phi Beta Kappa key, is an example of too much intellectualism. She was deprived of love as a child. Her mother worked from nine to five every day and her father, whose work as an editor required him to travel a great deal, was seldom at home.

"After I graduated from college, I found I disagreed too

often with my parents on religion and philosophy," June told me. "Religion left me cold. Determined to think things through for myself, I left home and for over a year traveled from one big city to another. I'd hold a good position for a while in one place, then, restless and miserable, I'd move on to a new city and another position."

"Did you find it difficult to secure new positions?" I asked.

"Oh, no, that was the least of my troubles, for I seemed to be able to do almost anything," she replied.

In a new city and a new place June would be extremely happy for a month, or sometimes even two months, but then she would be overcome with restlessness and would move on. Her health deteriorated, and she suffered from lack of appetite, indigestion when she did eat, headaches and loss of sleep. All these nervous symptoms made her miserable and suspicious of everyone. "In each place I would gradually become possessed with the feeling that I was violently disliked by those with whom I worked."

Her travels ended in New York. After only four weeks this time, she was again besieged by anxiety. One evening, too tired to sleep or eat, she left her YWCA room in search of a bookstore, hoping to find something to read. "My reason told me that I needed help and I decided that I would look up a doctor soon. In the bookstore, however, I saw a title that intrigued me, *The Power of Positive Thinking*. Leafing through the book I noticed it often referred to the Bible. I decided to buy a Bible and Dr. Peale's book."

"Did you find the book helpful?" I asked.

"No, it left me cold," said June. "The Bible didn't help, either. You see I was so rigid that I couldn't respond to them. I wanted to cry myself to sleep that night, but I couldn't cry. When I got up the next morning, I picked up Dr. Peale's book again and idly glanced at a few pages, then my eye caught the words, 'church clinic.' Before the day was over I phoned the church for an appointment."

After several private sessions, the Reverend Kew made her

a member of one of the clinic groups, whose functioning will be discussed later. June found she wanted to continue with the private sessions but Clinton Kew reminded her that she had agreed to do whatever was required for her health. At first she disliked the group and found it a painful experience because, she said, "I didn't like people and therefore couldn't love them. But I understood now that this was to be part of my therapy if I really wanted to be well and happy."

"How did you make out with the group?" I asked.

"Awful at first!" June laughed. "I'll never forget that first night. One of the girls in the group so irritated me that I shook in my effort to subdue the hostility I felt. At this point the Reverend Kew turned to me and said, 'You don't like Ann, do you? Some feeling you have repressed is now being felt.'

"I was embarrassed but I had to admit I didn't like Ann and although I was not aware of it then, this was the first real emotion I had felt for a long time."

"Why does Ann trouble you?" Clinton Kew continued.

Ginny, another college graduate from Rhode Island, spoke up. "Because June is jealous. I used to feel that way too, angry and afraid because I felt cheated. I wanted love but was afraid of it too. Underneath my anger and jealousy was a great need for love."

"My reasoning told me she was right," June explained. "I began to try hard to like people and as days passed into weeks, and then a year, I understood Jesus' words 'Thou shalt love thy neighbor as thyself.' I had to work out the anger within me before I could feel secure."

Although June had a good idea of what her problem was, she still had the bigger task of learning how to be warm like others, and then, gradually, to love, until the expression of that love brought the surrender of all she was and could be to those about her and to her God, whom she learned *was* Love.

"At the right stage of my development the Reverend Kew suggested I read the thirteenth chapter of Corinthians," she told me. "Many times since that first reading it has given me strength to keep on loving God enough to want sincerely to love people. I learned to cry, too, over that chapter but with tears of relief and joy." Then she repeated softly: "For God so loved the world, that He gave His only begotten Son, that whosoever believeth in Him should not perish, but have everlasting life" (John 3:16).

"So now you are all straightened out," I commented as we rose to leave.

"Oh, no," June quickly replied. "I believe I am in the process of being saved every day." Then, before I had a chance to agree, she was calling to a young woman about her own age.

"This is Ann," June told me, "who irritated me so violently the first night I attended the group."

They both told me of the friendship they now share, attending church on Sunday and the healing services, when possible, every Wednesday during their lunch hour.

"Oh, by the way, we do attend other functions outside the church and date together," Ann told me. "We belong to a college club." Then they went off together to another part of the church building for the coffee hour. In my heart I cheered them on.

In another group, I became interested in a man I will call James Stratmore, a businessman in his forties.

"You should have heard the gentle panning I took from my adopted family," he told me. "I was the oldest member of the group, but that didn't mean a thing to the college sophomore who said I was just like her know-it-all father who made their home life miserable."

"What brought that on?" I asked.

"Well, I had just finished spouting my views on this cockeyed world in general when she gave out with that comment. I felt like two cents and that went down to a half-cent when the others agreed."

"Did you answer her?"

"I was too angry to answer. I wanted to grab that youngster by the throat, but as the group continued to discuss my short-comings, I cooled off and remembered what Reverend Kew had explained to me in private. He said I could learn to handle my emotions if I would follow the advice of Jesus: ' "Agree with thine adversary quickly, whiles thou art in the way with him." There is no need to be on the defensive.'

" 'So we all agree that Jim is too domineering,' the Reverend Kew was saying.

" 'Then why do I act like this?' I asked the group.

"The answer floored me. 'You're insecure,' they said.

"Then I really thought they were all crazy," Jim Stratmore told me. " 'You're a bunch of neurotics and that's why you are here.' But this time I wasn't mad, just disgusted. I didn't know it then but that was my first sign of recovery."

As time passed James Stratmore began to see how right his adopted family was about him. He realized his excessive talking was a defense for not knowing the score. He felt important as long as he talked, even though he was ignorant of the facts involved.

"I learned to talk less, to study facts and read up on subjects so I could talk intelligently. Finally, my clinic family began to like me and I grew mighty fond of them. Incidentally, my own family began to notice the change and our love for each other deepened."

Jim Stratmore had first learned of the church clinic while attending a businessmen's annual banquet where Dr. Peale was the speaker. He was suffering from a severe case of colitis which several doctors had failed to cure. He recalled, as Dr. Peale spoke, that one of these doctors had told him, "I'm afraid, Mr. Stratmore, that only *you* can get rid of your colitis."

"I thought the doctor was just passing the buck," he said, "but as I listened I gathered Dr. Peale was saying much the same thing. I was down to zero because my business partner had told me off that day. He had shouted, 'What you need to learn is how to win friends and influence people the right way or we won't have any business left.' My partner, a quiet man, had never shouted at me or anyone as far as I knew. I felt like a heel."

The next day Jim Stratmore secretly visited the clinic and was introduced to the Reverend Kew. After a few private sessions, he was helped to realize that his trouble could be traced back to a quarrelsome childhood, one in which he was overridden by his parents. He had absorbed the insecurities of his family.

The most difficult part of his cure came with the joining of the clinic family. He had never gotten on with people but there he knew he must, or he would never be well or happy again.

"You know," he laughed, "I just hate not being in an adopted family, now that I'm well." Then he grew serious as he said, "Through psychotherapy and faith in a God of Love, I learned how to build my house upon a rock."

In church clinics across our country, normal men and women of all ages with overwhelming problems are learning how to live normal lives. They are learning to accept the problems that are beyond their power to change and to change those which can be remedied. Through religious psychotherapy normal people grow into a new maturity, thereby saving themselves from eventually drifting into the overpopulated ranks of the neurotics and psychotics. Jesus did not know the word psychotherapy, yet he applied it constantly in His ministry of soul-saving with such memorable phrases as "as a man thinketh in his heart, so is he."

The way to the Cross is not found without a painful struggle of the soul. I have gained great admiration for these people, of varied ages and occupations, who come together to accomplish the very difficult task of facing their problems in the presence of others, by learning how to lose their lives in order to find them.

Clifton Kew writes in *You Can Be Healed:*

> We can't make the world intelligible without God. Today, more and more psychologists are recognizing this need and are willing to accept the dependence upon a mature God as a healthy one. They have come to understand that such a dependence does not make people weak; it helps make them strong. Though religion does not take away the difficulties of life, it does teach man endurance and acceptance of them and how to surmount his selfishness. If religion were to spend more time building within its followers a love for God and man, and a sense of trust of psychological truth, there is no telling how far man could go in cleansing himself of mental and emotional disorders.

In the light of the experiences of people like June Andover and James Stratmore we know it is possible to cleanse our bodies as well. Jesus healed "all manner of sickness and all manner of disease among the people."

"Those who are healed in our clinic need no cloak. Religion is inside," Clinton Kew told me. "There is no resistance to God for they have submitted to Him, consciously and unconsciously, their minds, bodies and souls, and in so doing, have received a new life."

7 * LET'S GRIPE TOGETHER

Monday was damp, humid and unseasonably warm for November. I had accepted an invitation from the Reverend Clinton Kew to sit in on one of his "adopted family" groups, which I had learned a little about from James Stratmore. Eight men and women of various ages sat comfortably about in a reception room at the church clinic, much as they would in the living room of their own homes. The group is termed "adopted" by a few since that expresses the feeling some of the members have about the sessions. For the first time in their lives they are able to receive the kindly, but firm, understanding which they did not receive in their own families when they were children.

"Well, Bill, how do you feel this morning?" asked the minister-psychologist, turning to look at a dejected young man on his right.

"Not so hot," he answered in a lifeless tone. Then, somewhat sullenly, he added, "And I don't feel like talking either."

The minister smiled and said, "Who does feel like talking?" (I learned later that Bill was a young man who had spent a large portion of his early life in a strict religious school and who was not too comfortable in the clinic.)

"I do," piped up Alice, a pleasant-looking woman in her thirties. "My mother is driving me crazy and if I don't get it off my chest soon, you can send for the man in the short white coat to come and get me, as my teen-age son says."

The group members smiled—all but Bill. Alice went right on telling about her unhealthy emotional ties with her mother. She said that she was a grown woman now with three children and a very thoughtful husband, but that she was still unable to free herself from her mother's bonds.

"It doesn't matter what I do for Mother, she's never satisfied. I have done everything she has ever asked me, because she says it will make her happy, but it doesn't. My husband tells me to pay no attention to her, but she is my mother and I am not going to be angry at my mother. Yesterday I hung up the phone on her and an hour later I felt sick to my stomach and I was unhappy the rest of the day. When my mother doesn't call me I feel wonderful; but I worry if she doesn't call! I feel wonderful and then I feel bad. If she lived with us I would go nuts. I've tried to please her all my life, but I guess I can't." Alice began to cry as the tension of her frustrations mounted. She stopped talking.

Bill, who had refused to talk earlier, began to show more interest, and the story of Alice's feelings about her mother seemed to stir some hidden resentments within him. With considerable tenseness in his voice he asked, "Why do you, an adult, allow your mother to become such a threat? You can't live with her and you can't live without her."

"I know I'm acting like a child; like a little girl," Alice agreed. "I know I'm doing the same thing I did many times as a child, but I can't help it."

"You need not be afraid to express your anger here," said Clinton Kew with assurance. "That is why we are here."

"I realize that my mother worked hard after my father's death," Alice continued. "I know she is not to blame. She had to work hard to support us. She was often tired, cross and nervous and had a heavy load to bear. She had problems, too. Even though I know what I should do, I can't seem to do it. Some day I'll learn."

Bill was becoming more interested and he expressed his hostility by quoting from I Corinthians 13: "When I was a child I spake as a child, I understood as a child, I thought as a child: but when I became a man, I put away childish things." Bill became silent; the group was taking in every word he uttered. Finally he spoke again, "I feel like Alice. It is easy to quote the Bible; I had it rammed down my throat every Sunday." Bill looked up with surprise, for no one was angry or anxious because he was critical of religion.

Alice seemed relieved because it was apparent that the counselor, Bill, and the other members of the group understood her. She gained courage and strength. She didn't feel so much like a fool, or as guilty. Bill smiled; *his* tensions were reduced. With some anger gone out of both of them, the atmosphere was cleared of foggy thinking and Alice began: "I can see a way out. I can see the meaning of that passage. Part of my anxiety about my mother is within me. I can treat her like an adult . . . she is a person and I am a person, a grown-up person."

Alice spoke these words with feeling, she expressed a truth, but this time with a new feeling of acceptance and understanding. As the discussion continued, Alice faced her problem little by little and she began to realize that her strong resentment of her mother was due to the fact that she felt her mother didn't love her. Her hostility was a strong defense to her love needs.

"What do you plan to do when your mother calls again?" asked the Reverend Kew.

The clergyman knew that there was the very real problem of Alice's facing her mother as a person each time she called. He also knew, now that the resentment was boiling off, that Alice might hurt her mother again if she were not careful and the vicious circle of emotions would begin anew.

"The next time I talk with my mother," Alice answered, "I'll try to remember that she has a need for love too, and perhaps I can help her by loving her and treating her like a real person. I'll be more grown-up too, and it won't be as difficult to do now."

Bill smiled. He had grown a little too. He did not have that sullen, leave-me-alone look. Thus members of these family groups, unable to recognize their own problems, are capable of seeing them in others and through their help are able to resolve their own inner conflicts. And so step by laborious step, each member of the group made progress toward maturity. For Alice it was only a beginning. But it was a beginning.

As I sat in the group I was reminded of the words of St. Paul: "Let us run with patience the race that is set before us, looking unto Jesus the author and finisher of our faith" (Hebrews 12:1-2). Bill had felt the struggle within Alice and he was able to vent his feelings, something he was unable to do at the beginning of the hour. Each member would patiently meet his problems head-on, and little by little become free of the emotional and spiritual illness which made life so unhappy.

Mabel may suggest a nagging wife to Edward and the group will see Edward as he really is, a timid, insecure man who is afraid to stand on his own feet. As time goes by Edward will get a true picture of himself, resolve the inner frustrations, and will recall the experience of the past where the unfinished business of living is to be completed.

In addition to providing psychological insights into human behavior, the Reverend Kew helps people to become acquainted with the great passages from the Bible. Instead of the Bible's bringing them guilt feelings, anxiety and anger, as it used to do when they were forced to attend church, it now provides moral support and good sense. Many of the passages in the Gospels spring alive in the presence of these people who are facing the realities of life. There are no smug intellectual beliefs here, *the words are living in the people who speak them.*

"Many psychologists and psychiatrists, as well as clergymen, have more people coming to them for help than they can adequately handle alone," the Reverend Kew told me after the group session. "Because group sessions are possible for many people, one counselor can handle from six to eight people at one time over a period of many months. Several groups can be in session each week and it doesn't require any more time seeing the same number of individuals. Then, too, some people can be helped more rapidly in a group setting; they can elicit more responses from their past as they see the reactions of the other members of the group."

"How do those seeking help react to this?" I asked. "Wouldn't some of them prefer to have you to themselves for that hour?"

"Some people do not fit into groups," the Reverend Kew answered. "Others find it easier to ventilate their negative feelings in a group. They seem to secure a sense of protection from the other members and can express themselves more readily. Most of them like the idea once they get used to it. Usually when a person begins to feel better he prefers to be with a group. Group work is less expensive. Each person contributes, at the church clinic, whatever he can afford to pay. Those who have no income are not expected to pay. However, everyone wants to contribute to the work of the clinic in some way."

"How do you determine who will be in groups?" I asked. "I notice there were men and women of about the same age in some of the groups which I attended."

"Since most of our problems are derived from some phase of family life," he answered, "we try to form a new family of similar age range, with similar problems and with similar cultural background. The relationships between individuals in the homes of America are infinitely varied, and therefore it is not difficult to form groups with similar backgrounds and education. However, it is often wise to have one or two older people in a group to elicit responses from individuals who have a father or a mother problem, because these older people represent in some way the father or mother figure of the past. The younger individuals are able to understand their earlier conflicts and have an opportunity to 'live out' in a stable and friendly atmosphere their infantile lives and thus, without embarrassment, to see clearly and face their problems with complete frankness, just as people express themselves in a normal healthy family relationship."

"Isn't this a bit difficult to achieve, especially with a group of strangers?"

"Yes, at first," Clinton Kew replied. "But the group becomes a fellowship where one soon learns to take criticism as well as give it. This is the understanding when one joins a group."

"They might get in a fight," I said.

"This has never happened; they are not allowed to 'act out' their feelings. Instead of fighting or arguing as they did in their original homes, we ask them to 'talk out' their feelings, their beliefs and their conflicts. From the very beginning they are accepted by their adopted family for exactly what they are. So right away their egos are not threatened, but strengthened, and even the most reticent person will find it easy to speak. An older member of the group can help a new member to talk. That is, a person who has been in the group for a longer time and who may at first have suffered from extreme bashfulness can be very thoughtful and gentle in helping a new member who has the same problem to speak his mind. When fear and guilt are reduced, all can work together toward their common goal . . . a whole, healthy, personality.

"Would you like to sit in on the group that meets tonight?" the Reverend Kew asked me. "This group is a little different . . . it is made up entirely of college graduates. Two are Phi Beta Kappas, one is an engineer, another is with General Electric, two are section managers for large firms. One girl is executive secretary in a bank, another sales-promotion head of a fashion house."

That evening I met a group of young adults ranging in age from twenty-three to thirty-five who, because of accumulated frustrations through the years, had developed various physical illnesses and had come to the church clinic for help. In addition to some of these physical manifestations there were numerous mental and emotional problems. From their conversation I gathered that they knew one couldn't solve everything with "reason" alone. "Emotions," they said, were just as much a part of life as reason; man needed both and both should be expressed and work in harmony.

Jim, one of the young engineers, turned to a newcomer in the group and asked, "How do you feel this evening, Paul?"

"I feel guilty whenever I face the boss," Paul replied.

"Were you brought up in the fear of God *too*?" asked one

of the girls. Ruth smiled as she spoke. "Your boss is not God, you know." She seemed to sense that Paul didn't know why he was afraid. Strict authority seemed to be his problem.

"I am afraid of my boss . . . guess I give him powers he doesn't have." Turning to Ruth, Paul asked, "How did you know I felt this way?"

"Because that was my problem when I joined the group," Ruth admitted. "I had to obey my parents and I felt that if I didn't, God would punish me. My parents used to fight a great deal . . . they were cruel to each other. They were hard on me. I felt that God would be the same. I was making God in the image of my parents. God and cruel authority were the same thing to me. I had read that this often happened, but not until I experienced the freedom from facing my problem did I realize how strong this infantile concept really was."

"Paul will find it necessary to face up to it," said Marilyn. "Ruth knew she had done nothing to be guilty about and is now learning that her conscience was unrealistic in that it was too severe. It was a hindrance in her daily living. Now that her conscience has become normal and healthy, it will help her to live a more Christian life."

I learned later that as the weeks passed Paul regained his self-respect and found God, not with a club in His hand, but through Jesus' words, "As the Father hath loved me, so have I loved you: continue ye in my love. If ye keep my commandments, ye shall abide in my love; even as I have kept my Father's commandments, and abide in His love" (St. John 15:9-10).

Another member said that she was beginning to get closer to others. Because she was able to do so without being afraid, she was also feeling sympathy for the first time in her life. She was no longer afraid to feel sympathy, to give and receive it. I sensed that these young people were learning how to rid their lives of too much "self" and were beginning to be able to throw off illnesses of the body which were caused by their fears and anxieties, hatreds and jealousies, insecurities and guilts.

What had driven these people to the church clinic in the first place? I was given the rare opportunity of talking with several of the members of the group in private. They knew that I wanted to write something which might be of help to others, and knowing this, they were quick to respond to my request.

I knew that it was not easy for them to bare their feelings before others. However, since they were well on the road to living whole lives, they did not hesitate to talk with me. With God's help in the worship services and with their counselor's gentle and consistent leading, they were able to resolve their conflicts and talk with quietness and confidence.

One of them, Paula, sat before me in one of the small rooms of the church. I thanked her for coming to talk with me.

"I am happy to help in this way," she replied, "for I can't ever forget how desperate I was the first time I came to this church."

I knew that Paula was twenty-five years old and held an excellent position in promotion and advertising. She traveled widely and appeared on television regularly. It was difficult to believe this poised and delightful person could have been so desperately ill. I told her so.

"Oh, but I was!" she laughed, and then grew serious as she recalled the frustrated years when she sought peace and health.

"It was after college, when I began working for the firm I am now with, that I was afflicted with dizzy spells and weakness. I was extremely nervous and exceptionally thin for my age and height. My nervousness was also reflected in the cessation of my menstruation some years before. I got to the point where I didn't want to meet people and I knew that my position was at stake."

As a child Paula was intensely shy and fearful. She idolized her brother, who was tall and handsome. He had resented her arrival in the family as the "baby" who received so much attention. As a result, he sought little ways of tormenting her. He would pinch her and lock her in a dark closet when she was left in his care. These experiences were damaging to an overly sensitive little girl. Her brother also warned Paula not to tell her parents who, unaware of the true situation, often punished Paula for being afraid and shy.

"When I was sixteen," she continued, "my mother suddenly passed away. Just as suddenly my menstruation stopped. A year later my father died. My brother and I were reared by a relative until after our graduation from college. I felt lonely and unwanted. One day, when still in college, I went to the home of one of the girls. I couldn't believe that parents could be so kind, that the girl's older brother could be so thoughtful. I withdrew for years. I only kept up the contacts which would benefit my company, and then I only put on an act. I really shut people out of my life. The stopping of my menstruation seemed to be a symbol of my failure. I realize all this now, but then I had no idea that my illness was all in my mind."

Paula was wretched. Her spells of depression deepened and became more frequent. She sought help at several medical clinics but the doctors found nothing physiologically wrong with her. They tried to help her with various treatments which all failed. Several doctors suggested that maybe she ought to see a good psychiatrist.

"Then one Sunday morning," Paula told me, "I went to the Marble Collegiate Church and heard Dr. Norman Vincent Peale mention the clinic while telling a story about another girl who found new life and health there. I was in a bad way, with thoughts of suicide looming large before me. Life didn't seem worthwhile even though I had an excellent position and a good salary. I was alone and nothing was really interesting. Life had lost its purpose for me. On the surface I acted as if everything was perfect. Other people seemed to be genuinely happy and content. Why couldn't I feel that life was worth living?

"I had never heard of a church clinic before and Dr. Peale's sermon 'Cast thy burdens upon the Lord and He shall sustain thee' gave me new hope."

"How soon did you go to the clinic?" I asked.

"The very next morning I phoned for an appointment and learned the earliest date I could make was three weeks off. I will never forget the sense of despair that surged through me. I cried out 'Oh, I can't wait that long!' "

The secretary, who must have sensed Paula's desperation, gave her a noon appointment with the Reverend Kew. Paula was not put into a group at first, but met with Clinton Kew in private twice a week.

"At the conclusion of my first talk with Reverend Kew, I felt I had found my first ray of hope," Paula told me. "I thought of him as my kind brother to whom I could come whenever I felt desperate again. This made me a member of a new family. I was no longer alone. For the first time in my life I was able to be identified with someone and was able to receive the assurance and hope that religion gives. I also attended the healing services which Reverend Kew conducts."

After each session Paula left the clinic with less resentment; her confusion was slowly replaced by clear thinking. Love filled her heart where hate had been.

"During my sixth visit," Paula continued, "Reverend Kew quoted the Bible. This time he told me the story of the woman with an issue of blood and when he was finished he said, 'Paula, if God could heal this woman He can help you too.' I believed this and days later the change happened. My menstruation returned normally after a lapse of nine years. I understand now what deep-rooted hostility can do to one and I am really able to love people as I should. I learned to give up my anger, to love myself properly, and finally others.

"I feel I must continue therapy for another year to cleanse

myself of resentment, fear and guilt. Religion now gives me strength; it gives me courage because it offers new meaning through understanding. Especially did I feel love for my brother when I knelt in prayer in the church at the healing service."

The last time I saw Paula she was kneeling at the church altar during the Reverend Kew's healing service.

V

* * *

Healing Through

Pastoral Counseling

1 * THE MINISTER, ONE OF GOD'S HEALING CHANNELS

When Jesus sent out his twelve disciples, whom we recognize as the first Christian ministers, he first called them to him, and gave them power—"power against unclean spirits, to cast them out, and to heal all manner of sickness and all manner of disease." He also ordained them to "preach, saying, The kingdom of heaven is at hand" (Matthew 10:1,7).

From Jesus' day until the present ministers and all servants of our Lord have time and again experienced the power of the Holy Spirit to heal, in their own lives and in the lives of those they serve. Long before the word psychology came into our vocabulary it was nevertheless practiced. Jesus was in word and deed the best psychologist the world has ever known. His healing brought satisfaction to every troubled heart. Therefore it is the duty of every Christian minister and of the church to be prepared to meet the crises that arise in the lives of every human being. Today more persons are coming to their pastor or to some other church-sponsored center for help than ever before in the history of the church.

Here is a true account of how a trained minister counseled a professional man back to health and an active purposeful life of service. When a scientist we will call Dr. Clare Hansen finally learned about the Pastoral Counseling Service at Boston University he was in a hopeless physical condition; his mental outlook on life was thoroughly depressed.

During his first interview he revealed the facts concerning his health. He had a medical history of twelve years of ulcerative colitis accompanied by daily hemorrhaging. He had lost his job with a large company and could find no doctor who would take him as a potentially curable case. He was unhappy with his wife and family and was always tired. As his interviews with a trained pastoral counselor continued Dr. Hansen gradually began to realize that the troubles in his life dated back to the beginning of his illness. As time passed he was able to break away from the past and begin the long journey to a new outlook on life through surrender to God.

Dr. Hansen's interviews began in October and by the end of December all evidence of his colitis had disappeared, including the hemorrhaging. The following spring a complete examination showed no evidence of the twelve years of acute colitis, not even scar tissue. He wrote his counselor: "As a trained scientist, I must accept as clear proof of God's presence and love the fact of my physical healing. The love and understanding you have shown me has started to fill the void in my being and has given me the will to fight to win the battle with myself and the past."

He said that his own doctor was amazed at his recovery, and that he takes every opportunity to remind him that he has experienced a major miracle. Dr. Hansen is convinced that God performed the miracle through a pastor—the pastor who counseled him!

One of the most important duties of the Christian pastor is faithful visitation of the sick. The Christian church from the very beginning of its existence has been a sanctuary, for "the lame, the halt and the blind."

Jesus promised judgment to those who neglected the sick and the troubled and also promised great rewards to those who took up his commission: "Then shall the King say unto them on his right hand, Come, ye blessed of my Father, inherit the kingdom prepared for you from the foundation of the world: For I was an hungred, and ye gave me meat: I was thirsty, and ye gave me drink: I was a stranger, and ye took me in: Naked, and ye clothed me: I was sick, and ye visited me . . ." (St. Matthew 25:34-36).

A steadily increasing number of educational institutions concerned with the training of ministers are today teaching a whole new approach to illness and emotional disturbances through the study of the psychology of religion and through practical clinical training. The clergyman, as well as the doctor, needs a bedside manner and it is essential that a minister seek new methods that will help him better to understand those with whom he works and to mature more quickly through a better understanding of himself.

The Boston University School of Theology offers an excellent program of training, under Dr. Paul E. Johnson, head of the Department of Psychology of Religion. All theological students are required to take at least a three-hour semester course of clinical pastoral counseling. Many students work into their regular theology curriculum as many courses in psychology as their schedule allows. Others specialize, continuing in this field until they have received a Ph.D. in Pastoral Counseling.

In the following chapters we will see how ministers periodically lay aside their clerical robes to put on the white coat of the hospital attendant. In so doing they realize that there are religious needs in all illnesses, a need for faith, for meaning and a purpose in life, and for the courage to attain it.

2 * CLERICAL ROBE AND WHITE
INTERN COAT

As far back as 1927 there was clinical training for theological students at Worcester State Mental Hospital, with Chaplain

Anton T. Boisen, who also taught a course in Boston University School of Theology, assisted by one of the staff psychiatrists. The Reverend Carroll A. Wise, the chaplain's successor, continued this new approach with the teaching of a course in Religion and Health. When Dr. Paul E. Johnson came to Boston University he succeeded Professor Francis L. Strickland, who had been teaching pastoral psychology and had also correlated his teaching with Worcester State Hospital.

As chaplains began to return from the Second World War they brought with them a new urgency for training in pastoral psychology. Many of them were determined to take graduate work in counseling. The work grew steadily until today Boston University has one of the most complete programs for training in pastoral counseling in the country.

Classroom theory is applied in Boston-area hospitals. For the study of persons enduring physical illnesses, students spend the required semester hours either at Massachusetts Memorial Hospital or at Massachusetts General Hospital. Here they may work as orderlies, or may, under the chaplain's supervision, make sick calls upon patients, or both. They attend discussion groups at the hospital with the several chaplains and attend lectures by members of the hospital staff, which includes psychiatrists, social workers, nurses and administrators. The students write up their interviews and the papers are then brought to a supervisor for detailed analysis.

For the study of mental illnesses the students go to the Boston State Hospital or the Massachusetts Mental Health Center. Here is a typical program which might be followed at one of these institutions: Arriving at the hospital for the first session at 8:30 A.M., the student receives a half-hour briefing on the day's activities. He then attends lectures and sits in on staff discussions of specific cases. Each student is assigned to a particular patient, whom he sees for one hour each week; he is also free to talk with other patients as he visits the wards.

He writes a full report of these interviews and discusses them with his professor before his next visit to the hospital.

Any given student's activities vary according to the amount of clinical training he wishes to take. For instance, a young minister planning to do parish work (regular ministry in his own church) would not require as much clinical training as if he wished to specialize in order to enter the chaplaincy or become a pastoral counselor in a counseling service.

Nevertheless, many ministers in parish work are finding time to take courses in pastoral counseling when it is available in the area in which they live. Many more have given from six to twelve weeks of their summer vacation to clinical training, which is offered in many hospitals today.

During my visits to Boston University I have talked with many ministerial students, some new in the clinical-training program. One of these was Earl, who said, "Before I took this course the hospital world had been foreign to me, but now I feel like a solid citizen in this nation of uniformed servants. Before, I was terrified of those who were suffering and ill, but now I have a certain confidence in entering the rooms of the sick. Before, I was uncomfortable and mystified by those who handle and patch up the human body, but now I have come to accept and understand those who work at healing the flesh. Before, I was confused by the work of the minister in the hospital, but now I have learned to be more patient in waiting for the Lord to accomplish His work."

In class, the student discusses his hospital experiences with his professor to determine if he has acted for the good of the patient. If he has not, he learns where he can profit from his mistakes. He also sees at first hand how doctors work with clergymen to bring health to the patient in the hospital as well as in the pastor's study or the doctor's office. He takes satisfaction from the fact that he is free to call upon such trained professional persons as psychiatrists, social workers, marriage counselors and surgeons whenever he needs their help.

"Long before I was able to apply psychology," Peter, a second-year student, told me, "I had to learn such small things as how to enter a patient's room, not to sit on his bed or to jar it in passing, how to carry a bedpan. And I'll never forget the first time I had to rub a patient's back. I was embarrassed and uncomfortable, handling someone else's body with my bare hands, but then I thought of Jesus washing the disciples' feet and lost the feeling at once, for Jesus had instructed: 'If I then, your Lord and Master, have washed your feet; ye also ought to wash one another's feet.' I felt, also, a glow of satisfaction as the patient expressed his gratitude to me."

While performing the menial tasks of orderlies, students learn how to apply the psychology acquired at the university.

"One day," said Barry, another second-year student, "I found a business executive on my floor who was refusing to cooperate with hospital routine. He had suffered a heart attack and I sensed he was thoroughly disgusted with his apparent uselessness; his mental anguish was as acute as his physical distress had been a few days earlier. His doctor had forbidden him to raise his arms or exert himself in any way. This meant that the nurses had to feed him. The head nurse put his lunch tray in my hands and wished me luck. I sent up a quick S.O.S. prayer as I entered his room.

" 'You look very well, Mr. Manly,' I commented cheerfully.

" 'And I am well,' he replied tartly. 'But no one around here seems to think so! "Please Mr. Manly, don't lift your arm. Please, sir, don't wash your face. Don't get excited." Great scott, man, I'm an executive, not a baby!'

" 'It is hard to submit to such treatment,' I agreed quietly. 'But here I am with orders to feed you your lunch!'

"Then, before he had time to explode again, I said, 'Mr. Manly, I imagine you know how to save time, even days, when transacting business deals.'

" 'Of course, that's only good sense,' he replied.

" 'Then if you give this heart of yours as much rest as you can now, won't you save considerable time in getting back to the office?'

"He griped a little more, then smiled. 'You win, young man. Bring on the tray!' "

"Did he know you were a minister?" I asked Barry.

"No, not then, but when I passed his room later, he called me in and wanted to know what a bright young man like myself was doing as a plain orderly. Then I had to tell him that I was taking some clinical training to help me in understanding human suffering. He was much impressed with the program and the next week he had many questions to ask me."

I found that most of the theological students who trained in hospitals for the mentally disturbed enjoyed their contacts with mental patients and were of the opinion that they learned more about psychology from these patients than from the physically ill. One of these students, George, described his first day of clinical training to me.

After a briefing by the chaplain the students were told they could walk about the hospital and talk to anyone. "It was difficult to know which were the patients," George said. "Except for the violent cases everyone was free to walk about the corridors, or sit in the game room or watch TV in the lounge. I met a little man in the corridor and endeavored to pass the time of day. He smiled like anyone else and then he said, 'You're nervous, aren't you?' I was floored and speechless for a moment and then quite honestly I replied, 'I guess I am.' This patient made the same remark about me to the head chaplain who passed by us a moment later. I had been wondering if I had answered the patient as I should, so I was pleased to hear the chaplain say, 'I guess he is nervous.' "

When George had time to reflect, he realized that he had been nervous but had not been aware of it. For weeks afterwards he was known as "the nervous priest" by many of the patients. "It took some doing on my part to go back and face those patients every week."

But as George gained more training and experience he was no longer known as the nervous priest. He began to gain an insight and an understanding into human nature such as he had never known before.

"One day I was talking with a young college girl who had a deep guilt complex," George said. "She kept stressing the judgment of God, over and over, saying how much she deserved to be punished. Then in a moment of revelation I saw how she was using religion to condemn herself. At the same time I realized that she had forgotten the other aspect of God: forgiveness. When I suggested this idea to her she said, 'But why should God forgive me?' "

It was at this moment that George saw the full meaning of the Cross. He was then able to translate this great truth for his patient.

"God must judge us in order to forgive us," George concluded. "Yet God's love remains with us always so that we can become the person He wishes us to be."

"The patients respond to love and appreciate our visits," another student told me. "I visited a woman for eleven weeks and she didn't say a word to me. The twelfth week she talked about some of the things I had said to her. She asked me to sing 'Jesus Loves Me' with her and said I reminded her of God! 'And you and God love me. Thank you,' she said. I hated to say good-by to her at the end of my school year. I pray for her often and I know God worked through me to help her. On my last visit she asked me to sing with her 'What a Friend We Have in Jesus,' because I was like Jesus and He and I were her friends."

It is by learning to treat the patient as he would any other human being—without fear or embarrassment, whether his illness be physical, emotional or mental—that the student begins to understand compassion as Jesus knew it.

3 * BOSTON UNIVERSITY'S PASTORAL COUNSELING SERVICE

In 1952, because of the increasing interest and need for a counseling center, a suite of rooms was opened to the public in the Boston University School of Theology, under the direction of Dr. Paul Johnson and his colleagues. This project was made possible with the aid of a five-year grant from the Danielson Fund. The center is staffed by from eight to ten ministers, all trained in the psychology of religion. Students who are pursuing the requirements for a Ph.D. in Pastoral Counseling are required to do their intern counseling here.

The staff of counselors generally consists of two of the chaplains from the associated hospitals and eight professors from the Department of Psychology of Religion. Three consultants are also available when needed: a clinical psychologist, a social worker and a psychiatrist.

The counseling center grew out of a very real need. Students at the university and people in the Boston area were coming in to help for their problems, which in many cases were creating illnesses. It became necessary to establish a place where real help could be given in privacy. Ministers from the Boston-area churches also came for advice about difficult situations which troubled persons brought to them. Sometimes a minister found he could not help a particular person because that person did not recognize that his troubles lay within himself. Until such an individual could understand that he needed to change, the minister was helpless in guiding this soul.

A man came to his pastor one evening just after he had discovered that his wife and son had left him. He demanded that the pastor pray long and hard so that God would make his family repent and come back to him. His pastor knew that this man had driven his wife and son from him because of his domineering ways. Now he expected the pastor's prayer to change in one short hour the situation he had built up over the years. The pastor could only pray that this man, who obviously was suffering from hurt pride and loneliness, would become desperate enough to seek the help he needed. The pastor could then send him to a trained counselor for therapy.

The experience of Dr. Hansen, related earlier, is a further example of how emotional conflicts can wreck us, first mentally and then, so often, physically. Many such cases are helped each year at Boston University's Pastoral Counseling Service.

I talked with Dora, a pleasant middle-aged woman who had found healing through one of the pastors trained at the Boston center. "A year ago I was so sick I wanted to die," she told me. "I was unable to sleep a single night through without the aid of sleeping pills and then only rested in a semi-conscious state which always left me bone-tired."

Dora was highly nervous, suffered from a serious spastic condition, was addicted to eating and was thirty pounds overweight. The least excitement caused her to have migraine headaches. Mentally she had withdrawn from the world, hated everybody and screamed at her family continually.

"I finally lost my faith in God and believed I was an atheist," Dora said. "I had moments when I'd feel God's presence in a beautiful sunset, but it was a fleeting experience that always escaped me too soon. I continued to go to church but closed my mind to its meaning."

Then her husband's work necessitated their moving to another town. They joined a new church. The fellowship in the church was warm and friendly. Dora felt that the minister was concerned about her even though she had never revealed the seriousness of her condition to him or anyone. She learned that the minister had had training in pastoral counseling, something she had never heard of before, but she finally went to ask his help.

"How I got into the condition I was in then seems of no importance now, but I soon began to see that I was sorry for myself, mainly because I had married a fine man but one who was above my social level. This caused an inferiority complex which I could not overcome. Also I had been brought up in a home without love and with constantly quarreling parents. I began to see that I had never accepted my life as it was and that if I tried I might find my husband and children were really wonderful in themselves, if I did not try to make them what I thought they ought to be," Dora admitted.

After three months of weekly counseling with her pastor, Dora sat alone in the church, looking at the Cross in the chancel window. She sat for a long while in meditation. It was during the Lenten season and she longed to find the peace she now knew only God could bring to her weary soul.

"As I meditated on the meaning of the Cross, my faith was renewed," Dora said. "I had been reading from C. H. Dodd's book, *The Meaning of Paul for Today*. One paragraph held my attention as I read it over and over: 'The forces of evil drove Him through the horror of failure, scorn, agony of mind and body, dereliction of soul, and death in darkness. For all the storm He never bent or broke. It did not change His perfect self-surrender to God, or the purity of His love for those who did the wrong. Therein was the proof of His victory.' "

Dora went to the chancel and, on her knees, she too surrendered her life, promising to follow Christ's example as best she could. As she asked God to strengthen her, she found the peace she longed so to possess.

It was a joyful Easter for Dora and her family, who now understand her and help her. Her physical difficulties have all disappeared, and her weight and appetite are normal. Her pastor (who had, as we have said, received his counseling training at the Boston University School of Theology) stood by, rejoicing in her progress but letting her grow on her own as much as possible.

"Inwardly it is still a struggle at times even though I have successfully surrendered many of my old patterns of living to God," she told me. "Growing spiritually through Christ is to reach one plateau, only to see one farther on that must be reached. Mountain-top experiences, moments of loneliness and failure, loving people, learning to absorb hurts, finding God's will for my life—it is a day-by-day adventure with Christ as my guide."

Recently I received a letter from Dora in which she gave me a glowing account of her triumph over many little fears. At present she is holding down a very responsible church office position in order to help finance college educations for her children.

4 * MY PASTOR CARES

"Is this training necessary?" asked a young man who was contemplating where he would take his graduate work in preparation for the ministry. "When that question first began to trouble me I decided the answer could be found in someone who did think it essential and important enough to sacrifice for it."

That someone turned out to be a part-time student whom

we will call the Reverend Wesley Mann. Now in his thirties, serving a New England Methodist church, he carries a heavy schedule of pastoral duties as well as doing postgraduate work at the Boston University School of Theology. Despite this schedule he devoted many hours to interviews with me.

I wanted to know why he decided to take special training in pastoral counseling, and how it had helped his ministry.

"While serving my first church," Wesley told me, "I failed to help Jim, a young man who had just returned from combat duty in Korea. He was suffering from a deep depression caused partly by combat and partly by the shock of discovering when he returned home, that the girl to whom he had been engaged had married his best friend. Most of the time he sat about in stony silence, ate barely enough to keep alive and looked like a walking skeleton. His parents encouraged him to talk with me. I was only four years older than he and had already spent much time in prayer for Jim."

Jim finally came to church with his parents and began his talks with Wesley in the privacy of the study. Jim loosened up, talked more and began to think of finding a job. The young minister thanked God for these apparently good results. Then one day, without warning, Jim locked himself in his bedroom, muffled the pistol with which he had been taught to take enemy lives, and tragically took his own.

"I knew for the first time," Wesley recalled, "the agonizing pain of having failed one who needed spiritual help. I might have saved Jim's life if I had known then how to recognize and deal with a mentally depressed person."

Wesley began to take stock of himself. He had much to learn. He had an A.B., with a major in philosophy, from a university and a B.D. from Garrett Biblical Institute. Apparently this was not enough. Eventually he found his way to the Boston University School of Theology.

"Through the inter-related classroom clinical training and internship counseling, I am gaining a better understanding of myself," Wesley said. "Consequently my preaching has changed and now I am concerned with what people *feel* as well as with what they *think*."

Wesley learned that, while in days gone by the minister was expected to give advice, today a counselor will listen, let the person talk freely, telling his own story. The minister encourages confidence through understanding and sincere friendship, withholding advice until the troubled person releases his hatreds, guilts and anxieties, and begins to solve his own problems with gentle guidance from his minister.

"Mr. S., one of my church members, was contemplating a divorce, although I did not know it," Wesley recalled. "His wife was a semi-invalid who could hardly walk, and they had two growing children." One Sunday night Mr. S. came to church and was moved by the sermon. As he shook hands with Wesley at the door after the service he said, "That was a good sermon and I'd like to discuss it further with you some time."

Sensing a deep trouble, Wesley suggested that they take a little time right then. Mr. S. agreed, and the two went to Wesley's study.

They discussed the sermon for a while and gradually Mr. S. began to reveal his real problem. He was in love with another woman and said he felt the only fair thing to do was to leave his wife, whom he felt did not care for him any more. This was the beginning of many interviews between this man and his minister.

Wesley told me, "I did not start to tell him what I thought he ought to do, as I had Jim. I listened for many weeks while he poured out all his inmost desires, his hurt pride, his self-pity, until he realized that pride and pity had put him just where he was."

Slowly, with gentle guidance, Wesley helped Mr. S. to see the responsibilities he was running away from and to search his heart for his true love which he gladly admitted was for his wife and children. At length the evening came when the minister and Mr. S. could pray about the matter, and Mr. S. could go home to have a real talk with his wife.

It was then that Wesley began talks with both the husband and wife together. Mrs. S. now understands that her illness was psychological, and once her relationship with her husband became normal, her imaginary illness rapidly disappeared. Now they are the happiest, most useful couple in the church.

"I was able to introduce them in a new way to the Christ who has become their real Companion and Friend. Family worship and regular church attendance is an inspiring part of their family life," Wesley concluded.

Wesley's new understanding of marriage problems has made him an excellent counselor for young people.

His studies are not yet done. He is earning his Ph.D. degree in the field of pastoral psychology. It may take several more years, for Wesley is married, the father of two small children, and is serving a full-time church. But Wesley, like many other ministerial students, is not thinking about the hard work involved in carrying on his full-time church and part-time studies. He told me, "After four years at the university, I am still thrilled with the inter-related classroom and clinical training program."

In a world too fast and too frustrated it is heartening to know that ministers like Wesley are taking seriously the Biblical advice: "Get wisdom: and with all thy getting get understanding" (Proverbs 4:7).

5 * HEALING IN THE CHURCH'S CONSULTATION ROOM

Shuffling up New York's crowded Fifth Avenue, Tom Dale resembled a tramp in search of a hand-out. Few would have guessed that he had once been a successful salesman. None would have surmised that he was now headed for the famous Fifth Avenue Presbyterian Church, to keep an appointment with the minister, the Reverend Doctor John Sutherland Bonnell, famous throughout the world for his counseling work.

As he arrived in front of the church, Tom gazed up at the great stone structure and contemplated his situation. He did not want to see this minister and go over all his miserable failures again, but he had promised his wife, Doris, for the sake of their two children if not for himself, that he would at least talk things over with Dr. Bonnell. He doubted strongly if it would do any good, for no one could get him out of the mess he had made of his life. He was up to his ears in debt and out of work. No one would hire him and he couldn't blame them since he long ago had ceased caring about his appearance. He had promised Doris he would press his suit after she left for work but he hadn't enough gumption even to do that.

Finally, he sauntered around the corner and entered the 55th Street door to the church house. Waiting for the elevator which would take him up to the consultation room, just off Dr. Bonnell's study, he fought off the strong urge to turn and run. Months later Tom was to realize that the step he took into the elevator that day was the first right one he had taken in seven long years.

Alone in the consultation room, with five minutes to spare, Tom gradually became aware of his surroundings. His hands touched the Bible on the table before him. How long had it been since he had read it? His hand left the Bible to tighten, surreptitiously, his loose tie and to make a hopeless effort to smooth out his wrinkled suit. A picture on the wall engaged his attention. It was Holman Hunt's "The Light of the World," the painting of the figure of Christ, with lantern in hand, knocking on a locked door. Tom's thoughts were interrupted by the opening of a door, and Dr. Bonnell entered the room.

Tom Dale rose awkwardly to clasp the hand of the tall Canadian-born clergyman. Tom was surprised at the ease with which he was able to pour out his difficulties to this minister who inspired confidence and whose bearing spoke of a kindly understanding. Dr. Bonnell listened intently with no sign of the condemnation Tom had expected.

"I seem to have lost my grip on life and no wonder! How would you feel if you had been the second highest seller out of sixty salesmen and, when the company changed hands, been let out just like that?" Tom trembled with resentment. "I haven't been able to sell anything since and my nerves are all shot. I'm only forty-three, so why can't I get on the ball again?"

By listening patiently and by interjecting an occasional comment or question, Dr. Bonnell was able to lead this man, after weeks of counseling, to the realization that the answer to his problem would come as he began to face up to life alone without help from anyone. When he could stop feeling sorry for himself, he would be able to work to achieve the joy that comes with success.

As he gradually learned the reasons for his defeat, Tom was able to start the battle of overcoming them. For instance, when his father died, his mother had become overprotective in her relationship with her small son. She made life as easy as possible for him, solving all his difficulties and denying him the right to play at rough games because she feared he would be injured. When he married, in his thirties, she planned the wedding and now, during his unemployment, she was aiding him and his family with funds from her hard-earned savings.

His most helpful discovery came when he realized that his religious life was found wanting. He was praying that God would solve his problems. Now he found an inner peace as he sought strength from God to solve those problems himself. Dr. Bonnell, who often uses the Bible as a guide, one day referred Tom to Philippians 4:13: "I can do all things through Christ which strengtheneth me."

After that Tom went back to his own church where he attended services with his family every Sunday. Soon he was elected to the Ushers' Association and made such an excellent suggestion for improvement that the ushers unanimously made him head usher. A business executive who was a member of the church, was also impressed and offered Tom Dale a responsible position in his firm. Before this time he had taken a menial job, the only one he could find, determined to stick it out with Dr. Bonnell's encouragement, to make good at it until something else came along. Now he had his big chance.

"I kept repeating, 'I can do all things through Christ which strengtheneth me,' whenever I was afraid I couldn't make the grade," he said. Today Tom is in charge of the entire sales force of a large business house.

Tom Dale's story, and those of others, are told in Dr. Bonnell's books, *Psychology for Pastor and People* and *No Escape from Life.*

Dr. John Sutherland Bonnell has over thirty years of pastoral counseling to his credit. His successful use of spiritual therapy is firmly rooted in Christian psychology.

During my interviews with him he told me of his early interest in this field. His father, who supervised a large Canadian mental hospital, occasionally permitted his son to visit the institution with him. Deeply impressed, John Bonnell at the age of seventeen volunteered his services as a male nurse in this hospital and was accepted. For nearly three years he worked under the supervision of the medical director of the hospital. The desire to help people grew within John until he became aware of a definite call to serve God in the Christian ministry. By the time he had finished his college and seminary preparation and was finally established as a minister in his first church he had acquired considerable insight in counseling.

It was unusual in that day for a clergyman to have pastoral counseling training; courses of that type were very rare.

As the science of psychiatry grew, Dr. Bonnell grew with it. He read books on the subject and gradually came in contact with prominent men in the field. When he answered the call to the Fifth Avenue Presbyterian Church, he found the city of New York offered him a real laboratory in which to test his skill and continue his growth.

The fact that many of our physical illnesses are caused by our wrong attitudes is widely accepted today. Dr. Bonnell has helped to bring healing to many through the use of spiritual therapy. He told me of three sisters who lived in a constantly brewing caldron of malice caused by Jane, the youngest of them, who was a helpless cripple. One of the sisters wrote Dr. Bonnell that they had been listening to his radio broadcasts for several months and felt sure he could cure their sister. They had finally succeeded in convincing her that she should talk with him.

The three sisters drove many miles to New York and remained there for several consultations with Dr. Bonnell. Jane soon learned the causes of the resentment which was largely responsible for her illness. Against her will she had been compelled to give up her teaching position to take care of her sick father when her mother died. Years later, when he died, her two widowed sisters moved into the homestead with her, because the father had willed it to them, leaving her only $100. Jane dwelt upon this injustice until self-pity won her over. She really believed that no one loved her, certainly not her father or her sisters or God. Then she suffered a stroke and her sisters were beside themselves trying to please Jane, who was constantly irritable.

During her first consultation with Dr. Bonnell she spent most of the time complaining about everything in general. Finally Dr. Bonnell began in a quiet but firm voice to read the Bible to her. She tried to ignore him, continuing her discourse, but finally she began to take in the meaning of his

words: "Love suffereth long, and is kind; love envieth not
. . . Doth not behave itself unseemly, seeketh not her own,
is not easily provoked, thinketh no evil . . ." (I Corinthians
13:4-5).

By the end of the third session, as Dr. Bonnell and the
three women prayed, Jane had found a faith. At the moment
of departure, when her sisters tried to help her, she waved
them aside with a smile. Then, turning to Dr. Bonnell, she
raised her hand to him and said, "Will you please take my
hand?" As he did so she grasped it firmly and then, to the
astonishment of all, raised herself from her wheel chair and
walked to the elevator assisted only by Dr. Bonnell's hand at
her elbow. It was the first time she had walked in two years.

Every now and then a letter reaches Dr. Bonnell from the
sisters, who now enjoy their life together. In one of Jane's
letters she said, "I'll always be grateful for one of the Bible
verses you gave me, 'Let all bitterness, and wrath, and anger,
and clamour, and evil speaking, be put away from you, with
all malice: And be ye kind one to another, tenderhearted, for-
giving one another, even as God for Christ's sake hath forgiven you. Be ye therefore followers of God, as dear children;
And walk in love, as Christ also hath loved us . . .' " (Ephe-
sians 4:31-32; 5:1).

If you think the world owes you a living, you might study
Hoffman's picture of Christ in Gethsemane as Beatrice Tree
did. While she poured out the long list of her heartaches to
Dr. Bonnell her eyes wandered again and again to this picture
on the wall facing her. Presently she broke off speaking in the
middle of a sentence. She could no longer take her eyes away
from it. Dr. Bonnell also turned to look at it. After a long
moment of silence the minister quietly said, "Life has been
hard on you, hasn't it?"

"Yes," she answered.

Then, nodding toward the picture, he said, "It wasn't exactly easy on Him, was it?"

"No, it wasn't," she replied.

From then on they talked about some of Christ's heartaches and remembered that He managed to triumph over each one as He trusted His Father in Heaven to help him. Beatrice, who a few minutes before had been blaming the church and religion for not helping her, now overwhelmed by shame, said, "Oh, I didn't think of *Him* when I criticized the church."

After three months of spiritual therapy Beatrice changed from an unattractive, bitter woman into a glowing personality who now gives all her free time in service to the church.

Dr. Bonnell believes we all need a course in how to live; and he knows no better way than through the guided spiritual therapy that only the church can offer.

If you have not found an abundant life which comes from inner peace, then why not think over carefully these three considerations, which Dr. Bonnell believes are the chief causes of failure in life:

1. Lack of purpose. Ask yourself, "Have I a clearly defined goal in life?"

2. Lack of ability to see life through to a good finish. "Do you have staying power?"

3. Unwillingness to see one's own faults. "Are you willing to consider and try to overcome your faults?"

If you would like to be a better person, here, very briefly, are some points to ponder:

1. Be willing to admit your weaknesses.

2. Be patient with the mistakes of others.

3. Put yourself in the other fellow's place before you judge him.

4. Know yourself and God.

5. Discover the healing power of Love.

6. Learn to discipline yourself in order to gain a mature spiritual life. Seek communion with God every day through reading the Bible and in unselfish prayer.

VI

* * *

Think on

These Things

1 * WHY DOES GOD ALLOW SUFFERING?

Certainly God could stop all suffering at once. We do not understand why he brings healing to some and not to others; why some with great faith must continue to suffer while others without faith and sometimes not deserving of God's healing are, nevertheless, healed.

During his own ministry on earth, Jesus healed the unworthy with the worthy. Only one of the ten healed lepers returned to express his gratitude, and Jesus healed the ear of the servant of the high priest even while he assisted in Jesus' arrest, in the garden of Gethsemane. We must remember that Jesus' purpose in healing the sick was not solely to cure the body but to point the way to saving the soul, to teach us how to find abundant life on earth. He came to prove that the way was through Him, the Son of God. "I am the way, the truth, and the life. . . ." He longed to show man that his soul was the place where healing was needed. In St. Matthew 16:26 we read, "For what is a man profited, if he shall gain the whole world, and lose his own soul? or what shall a man give in exchange for his soul?"

Those who have suffered know that it is not always in vain, for out of infirmities and distress often come strength and maturity, wisdom and understanding; and, with those who trust in God, a closer fellowship with Him is the best reward. Paul, who was thrice denied healing, even though he served

God faithfully, was able to write: "We glory in tribulations also: knowing that tribulation worketh patience; and patience, experience; and experience, hope: And hope maketh not ashamed; because the love of God is shed abroad in our hearts by the Holy Ghost which is given unto us" (Romans 5:3-5).

During my visit with the late Fulton Oursler, the distinguished author of many religious books (*The Greatest Story Ever Told*, *The Precious Secret*, among others), he related the following story of a man whom he had interviewed in a small village in France.

"I began wondering what happened to people who are not healed," said Mr. Oursler. "For instance, it is a known fact that only five per cent of those who visit the shrine at Lourdes are actually healed. Yet many who make the pilgrimage make tremendous sacrifices, involving finances, physical endurance and emotional crises."

Mr. Oursler's search for the answer led him to the officials, both doctors and priests, in charge of the records of the pilgrims to Lourdes. He received names and addresses of many who had apparently come away from the shrine disappointed and unhealed. In a small village in France, Mr. Oursler found one of these—a middle-aged man, the victim of paralysis which left him flat on his back, able to move only his neck and head. He could, however, talk and his eyes and facial nerves were normal.

"I wondered why he had sent word for me to call at his home at eight o'clock in the morning," Mr. Oursler told me. "It still puzzled me as I stood looking down at this man on his stretcher bed. He greeted me kindly and asked me to be seated.

"Not knowing how long or short the interview might be I plunged directly into the reason for my visit. I asked, 'My friend, you were not healed at Lourdes, now what?'

"His face broke into a beautiful smile as if he were remembering a pleasant experience, then looking directly at me he replied in a quiet but happy tone:

" 'Oh, but God did heal me. You don't understand. Sit down and let me tell you about it. My wife and I sacrificed everything we could sell to raise enough money for the pilgrimage. Friends were wonderful, helping us to prepare for the trip and adding their gifts also. The trip on the train was long and trying and when I finally found myself before the shrine, bitter thoughts possessed me. What had I to live for? I was in debt and the possibilities of ever earning enough money to support my wife and myself were hopeless. One of those overwhelming depressions had caught up with me again. I cried out, "Lord, help me—help me solve my problems!"

" 'Then as I lay there in the warm morning sun, I began to think that maybe God had a plan for even such as I and that was why he let me live.'

"His face glowed," said Mr. Oursler, "—glowed as if the memory of it all had become a precious secret enshrined in his heart. He said, 'Suddenly I was alive with the assurance that all would be well again. On the train home my wife and I compared notes and she too had felt this glorious uplift of spirit. We felt a peace we had not known for several years.

" 'At home I awoke the first morning feeling rested and filled with a sense of expectation. I lay there, just thanking God for the happiness he had given us. Then God began to put an idea into my head. You are going to write a book! Just like that, as if I had written dozens before. Then just as suddenly I knew that if God wanted me to write a book, I could and would. My wife and I talked long and earnestly about it and then got to work. There were days when thoughts came in abundance and we studied and we wrote again and finally the book was about finished. One of our neighbors wrote to a publisher in London who came one day and took our book back to his editor, who accepted it. It had a good sale which enabled us to pay our debts and to meet our needs a while longer.

" 'Now God had another reason to keep me living. When

He said I was going to teach school, I wasn't even surprised, for both of us knew we could do anything with our Lord beside us.'

"Our conversation was interrupted by the ringing of a bell outside the house. Soon children were scampering about in another room. The courageous wife of this victim of paralysis came to wheel her husband on his stretcher into an adjoining room. I followed them and found a small schoolroom equipped with desks and blackboard. I stayed until the morning recess, fascinated, watching the husband teach while his wife assisted at the blackboard. I rose to express my gratitude before leaving. I learned that at first the village people were afraid to send their children for fear that they would catch his sickness. But the two doctors in the village settled that by sending their children first. With teachers all too scarce this so-called 'handicapped' couple were of real service to their village."

I had forgotten for the moment that I was in Fulton Oursler's study, so engrossed had I become as he told me this inspiring story. He concluded by saying,

"Once more I stood looking down at this courageous man. How could I let him know of my admiration? I wanted to clasp his hand but knew he would not feel the warm pressure of mine, so I looked for a long moment into his brave eyes. He held my gaze, smiled and said,

" 'You see, Mr. Oursler, God gave me the greatest of all healing—he healed my mind and heart and soul.' "

If we accept our infirmities and our suffering and the life we cannot change and give it to God, striving to obey His will, He will give us abundant lives, and the "peace that passeth understanding." We cannot know why God answers some of our prayers in ways we least expect, but He has not asked us to be concerned at this point. He asks only that we trust Him. There are times when God does reveal Himself to us if we are willing to discipline our souls to an awareness of His presence within us.

THINK ON THESE THINGS

Some of us are not healed and continue to suffer because we bring on our own misery and pain. During my service as a Gray Lady I met a patient, a woman of fifty-two, who was facing a radical breast operation, although she had not been told how serious her condition was. Her surgeon asked me to talk to her before the operation.

"If you can alleviate some of her fear it will help all of us," he said.

I found her alone in her room. She told me her husband could not leave his business to be there for the operation, but would be in that evening. No one else was there either. I felt sorry for her because she was frightened and alone. At her request I promised to stay with her as much as possible that morning and to wheel her up to the operating room. I listened as she talked of her fears. Then she added, "I wish I'd gone to church more, and I can't pray. I've been trying to think of a prayer to say. All I can think of is, God help me!"

"That's enough," I assured her. "God will be near you and I will pray for you all during your operation."

My heart ached for this woman but as I listened to her that morning, I began to feel sorry for her husband also. Her teeth had been neglected for years, and when she smiled the cavities and yellowed teeth were not pleasant to look at. Her hair was thick and must have been beautiful but now it was frizzy with a permanent that had never been set, or so it seemed. She was thirty pounds overweight and looked as if she were nearing seventy.

I was with her most of the morning and took her to the operating room. Her fears had subsided and the drugs had done the rest. The operation was successful—as successful as was humanly possible, for the cancer was in an advanced stage. She had only a year to live.

I prayed earnestly for her for weeks. Fear had conquered her. Had she gone to church and tried to find God's peace within herself, she might have conquered that fear. One afternoon I met her husband, an attractive and friendly man, suc-

cessful in business and considerate of those who served his
wife. After her operation her color returned, she lost some
weight and one could see that she had been pretty, and still
could be—had it not been too late.

We talked of God's healing power and she asked for a
Bible and began to read it for the first time since she had
been a child in Sunday School. God certainly did not bring
that suffering upon her. So many times in the last weeks she
would say to me, "Oh, why didn't I have that operation six
years ago? It's my own fault. And I'm going to the dentist
when I am well again."

I wanted God to heal her, to give her another chance, for
He had healed others like her. But who are we to say that
God did not heal her? She surrendered herself to Him several
months before her death, even though she died in agony from
the gnawing pain that drugs could no longer smother. In
death she found release and in Christ a blessed peace.

God has placed within us all kinds of power to use in making our lives strong in trouble, radiant in loving service, and
it matters little what life may bring in the way of sorrow. We
can take it! "For when God is for us, who can be against us?"

God never promised that life would be easy. Jesus told His
followers, "In the world ye shall have tribulation: but be of
good cheer; I have overcome the world."

2 * WHAT CAN I DO TO BE HEALED?

Suppose you do not live near a church where healing services
are available. Suppose you do not know where to find a prayer
fellowship that could pray for you. Perhaps you live out in

the country many miles from a church clinic. Or, if one of these healing centers is available, you are physically unable to reach it. What can you do?

I would not presume to tell you what you should do. You alone must decide what method of help you feel you can honestly accept. From those who have shared their experiences with us through this book, we have learned that God heals in various ways. Some were healed by divine power, which we call the supernatural. Others God healed with the help of—or through—doctors, medicine and hospital care. Some were only partly healed and some were not healed at all.

I have asked myself many times what I would do if I were in need of physical healing. If I were in complete control of my mind, this is what I would do: First, I would talk it all over with my Lord, whom I love and trust with my whole being. This love and trust is evidence of my complete surrender to His will for my life. I would tell Him all about my illness even though He would already be aware of it to a far greater degree than I. I would turn over my burden of suffering to Him. I would promise to leave my illness in His capable hands. I would ask God to pardon my sins. Then, I would ask for His healing power for my recovery. This is the asking part of my prayer and it would not be necessary for me to repeat it. I would endeavor to keep my mind free of my illness as much as possible so that I could devote myself to others.

Secondly, I would praise God daily for the blessings I have from His hand. I would thank God, first of all, for His Redeeming Love and for the Bible which each day helps me keep His presence in my heart. Although I know there are many contradictions in the Bible because of the human hands that have transcribed it, I would nevertheless pursue Paul's advice: "Study to shew thyself approved unto God, a workman that needeth not to be ashamed, rightly dividing the word of truth" (II Timothy 2:15). I would believe that in so doing God would reveal the great truths of the Christian life to me, for Jesus said: "Seek ye first the kingdom of God, and His righteousness; and all these things shall be added unto you." Jesus was referring to the spiritual side of man when He uttered these words in His Sermon on the Mount. The whole sermon deserves thoughtful study and is an excellent pattern to practice when bringing man's soul to a meeting place with God. In worshiping God I would also thank Him not only for my family and friends who love me as I love them, but for the compassion he has placed in my heart for all human beings, and I would seek His guidance in using this compassion.

Thirdly, I would avail myself of all possible help; that is, all that I can honestly accept and believe in according to my Christian beliefs. I would gratefully call upon my minister, seeking his spiritual guidance and prayers, and at the same time I would call upon my physician, who has taught me the value of preventive medical care. I would be as active physically as possible and *I would try to do the impossible with God's help.*

I would not be concerned about how God would heal me; rather I would endeavor to keep in mind constantly that God was healing me. This is the three-point program I would follow with God's help, and I cannot help feeling that God would do the impossible, "For in Him we live, and move, and have our being."

"Oh, yes, that's fine," you may be saying, "but just you wait and see what happens when you are consumed with pain and despair. Then you will sing a different tune."

I agree with you that at this moment I do not know what I would do. I only know what I think I would do. However I am sure that as I continue to *think these thoughts*, while in health, that they would become a part of my subconscious in illness.

Let me tell you about a young woman who found healing through discipline and faith. As a member of the Altar Com-

mittee of my church, it is my duty, during certain months of
the year, to arrange the altar flowers for the Sunday services.
One Saturday afternoon as I worked at the altar I heard faint
sounds as if someone were crying. I walked down to the
chancel, which was partly obstructed from my view by the
pulpit. There I found Jane Keiper Maraska on her knees in
prayer trying to muffle the sobs that shook her body. I knew
this young woman only by sight for she was not, at that time,
active in the organizations of our church that would have
brought us together. I knelt beside her until she became aware
of my presence.

Surprised, she cried, "Oh, Mrs. McKelvey, what can I do?
What can I do?"

"Whatever your problem may be it is not too big for God
to solve," I answered.

Later we sat in the choir pews to the left of the divided
chancel, where we could see the tall, softly lighted Cross on
the wall above the altar. This is the place where our small
prayer groups meet regularly and for me it has become a
place hallowed by prayer.

Jane's hair was cut short, for she was wearing a large,
thickly padded cervical collar which the doctor recommended
for easing the pain in her neck and shoulders. She suffered
from a progressive numbness which had localized in her hands
and arms. The pain in her neck and shoulders was constant.
X-rays had failed to reveal the cause of this pain. However,
one electric impulse test showed positive at the base of the
neck, indicating possible damage to three nerve roots.

Jane was handicapped physically in many little ways, but
she told me that she wanted more than anything to be able
to lift her baby without pain. She had been forced to take the
baby to her mother where he would receive proper care. She
could not drive her car, either, and found the ugly collar
cumbersome.

"If I could just do these three things, lift my baby, drive
the car and be able to go without this collar," Jane said, "I'd

be so grateful. You said nothing was impossible for God to do. Then why hasn't He answered my prayers?"

Her earnest young face turned to me, unguarded in that searching moment, and revealing the agonizing despair she suffered. I answered, "Jane, I know God wants to answer your prayer but sometimes even good church members like you and me don't know how to pray. I'm still learning how."

Then I suggested we ask God's help first. I prayed briefly that God would surround Jane with His love and bring her peace and healing. Then I asked for His Guidance and I thanked Him.

Jane was a graduate nurse and it suddenly occurred to me that she had been holding in her mind a vivid picture of those three nerves in the back of her neck, which *she knew* were the cause of her trouble. We discussed this briefly. I reminded her that since the doctors did not really know what the cause of her illness was, perhaps she shouldn't be so positive that she knew. I asked her to forget this picture, to erase it as soon as possible from her mind.

"God knows all about your trouble," I assured her, "and no one else needs to know. Right now give all your trouble to Him. 'Cast thy burden upon the Lord, and He shall sustain thee: He shall never suffer the righteous to be moved.' "

Two days later Jane came to the parsonage and we mapped out a plan much like my three-point program for discipline, except that we added a new idea that came as we talked together. She decided for the next two weeks to list her thoughts under two headings: Negative and Positive. At first the negative list was longer than the positive, but gradually, as her prayer discipline continued and she became more and more aware of God's presence in her life, the negative list dwindled. This does not mean that Jane never had a negative thought after that, but it does signify that the negative thoughts are not entertained in her mind for any longer than it takes to wipe them out by replacing them with affirmations of faith.

At the end of two weeks Jane drove her car to church! She looked like a different person without the cervical collar. Her face was radiant as she told me, "I'm making a few important discoveries. One is that I have been so full of my troubles that I lost interest in everyone else. Now other people and their happiness bring me real pleasure. I had a chance to cheer up a friend yesterday. In my daily reading the Bible is alive with new interest and the devotional books help me to understand that suffering can be a blessing."

Jane spent the next week learning all over again how to pick up pins with fingers not yet completely free of numbness. Her four-year-old son was a constant joy and comfort, but she longed for her nine-month-old baby. She was willing to pay the price in effort, praying as she set herself small tasks: "Dear Father, I'm going to hold this glass of water level and then carry it. With Your help I will have the courage and strength to do it."

Jane learned to sew again and to set her hair with bobby pins. By the end of the month, with these accomplishments to her credit—plus only a mild pain in her neck—Jane felt she was ready to send for her baby boy. One day she phoned me to say, "Mother is on her way here with our baby. Pray that I will be able to lift him."

Nothing could stop Jane now! I knew she would meet this final test as she had the others. Later she told me what had happened. When her mother arrived she placed the baby on the floor and Jane watched him creep happily about. She longed to pick him up but was still afraid to attempt it. She was afraid, afraid the severe pain in her neck and shoulders would return from the strain of lifting. She prayed, "Lord, I know I should not be fearful and I should not ask you for a sign, but if I am going to be able to take care of my baby, let him start to walk now." The baby sat still for a moment, then got up on his feet and walked toward her, proudly taking his first steps. Overjoyed, she caught him up in her arms, un-

aware that she had lifted him until suddenly she was holding
him without a trace of pain.

It is significant to note that Jane joined a prayer group of
five young women, all mothers of small children. The prayer
fellowship shared with this group was a therapy which continued to strengthen Jane as she realized that others of her
own age group, with like interests, were also seeking spiritual
maturity. Jane and her husband, John, give as much time as
they can in service to our church. Jane served for two years as
Spiritual Life Chairman of our Woman's Society of Christian
Service.

She relinquished this position some months before the
birth of her third child, which was the little girl she had always wanted. When I visited her at the hospital she said,
"What a different attitude I had during this pregnancy and
delivery."

I recently received a letter from Jane. She wrote, in part: "I
find that life is now an adventure of quiet joy. I feel that my
soul had to reach up to God in a kind of faith I never had
before. When I was able to feel His presence again and again
as I practiced my spiritual setting-up exercises, I came to call
them discipline. Only then did God's power begin its work
within my body. Along with the spiritual setting-up exercises
I had to make every effort to do the things that had to be
done, such as lifting heavy cooking utensils. But God always
gave me the strength to do it when I showed Him I had the
faith to go ahead. I shall never be worthy of His rich blessings
but I shall never stop trying!"

Love is the secret—God's love is the power. We need to
recondition our minds concerning spiritual healing. God is
waiting for us to discover and use love's healing power which
he has placed in every human heart. In order to make possible
this love for us He gave His life. For this greatest of all gifts,
what will you give?

A READING LIST

Bach, Marcus, *They Have Found a Faith*, Bobbs-Merrill Co., Inc.

Banks, John G., *Healing Everywhere*, St. Luke's Press.

Beard, Rebecca, *Everyman's Goal*, Harper & Brothers.

————, *Everyman's Mission*, Harper & Brothers.

Bonnell, John Sutherland, *Psychology for Pastor and People*, Harper & Brothers.

————, *No Escape from Life: Leaves from a Counselor's Casebook*, Harper & Brothers.

Cabot, Richard C. and Dicks, Russell L., *The Art of Ministering to the Sick*, Macmillan Co.

Carrington, W. L., *Psychology, Religion and Human Need*, Channel Press.

Clapesattle, Helen, *The Doctors Mayo*, University of Minnesota Press.

Clark, Glenn, *How to Find Health Through Prayer*, Harper & Brothers.

————, *I Will Lift Up Mine Eyes*, Harper & Brothers.

Daily, Starr, *Love Can Open Prison Doors*, DeVorss & Co.

————, *Recovery*, Macalester Park Publishing Co.

Day, Albert E., *An Autobiography of Prayer*, Harper & Brothers.

Dunbar, Flanders, *Emotions and Bodily Changes*, Columbia University Press.

————, *Mind and Body: Psychosomatic Medicine*, Random House.

Fosdick, Harry Emerson, *On Being a Real Person*, Harper & Brothers.

Germain, Walter, *The Magic Power of Your Mind*, Hawthorn Books, Inc.

Gross, Don, *The Case for Spiritual Healing*, Thomas Nelson & Sons.

Haggard, Howard W., *Devils, Drugs and Doctors*, Harper & Brothers.

Hutschnecker, Arnold A., *The Will To Live*, Prentice-Hall, Inc.

Johnson, Paul E., *The Psychology of Pastoral Care*, Abingdon Press.

————, *The Psychology of Religion*, Abingdon Press.

Jones, E. Stanley, *Is the Kingdom of God Realism?*, Abingdon Press.

Kelly, Thomas, *A Testament of Devotion*, Harper & Brothers.

Kew, Clifton E. and Clinton J., *You Can Be Healed*, Prentice-Hall, Inc.

Künkel, Fritz, *In Search of Maturity*, Charles Scribner's Sons.

Liebman, Joshua L., *Peace of Mind*, DeVorss & Co.

Lurton, Douglas E., *The Power of Positive Living*, McGraw-Hill Book Co., Inc.

Marshall, Catherine, *To Live Again*, McGraw-Hill Book Co., Inc.

Maves, Paul B., ed., *The Church and Mental Health*, Charles Scribner's Sons.

McNeill, John T., *A History of the Cure of Souls*, Harper & Brothers.

Menninger, Karl A., *Man Against Himself*, Harcourt, Brace & Co.

Menninger, Karl A. and Jeanetta L., *Love Against Hate*, Harcourt, Brace & Co.

Moseley, J. Rufus, *Perfect Everything*, Macalester Park Publishing Co.

Oates, Wayne E., *The Bible in Pastoral Care*, Westminster Press.

————, *Religious Factors in Mental Illness*, Association Press.

Overstreet, Harry A., *The Mature Mind*, W. W. Norton & Co., Inc.

Peale, Norman Vincent, *The Power of Positive Thinking*, Prentice-Hall, Inc.

————, *Stay Alive All Your Life*, Prentice-Hall, Inc.

————, ed., *Inspiring Messages for Daily Living*, Prentice-Hall, Inc.

Rhoades, Winfred, *The Self You Have to Live With*, J. B. Lippincott Co.

Roberts, David E., *Psychotherapy and a Christian View of Man*, Charles Scribner's Sons.

Sanford, Agnes, *The Healing Light*, Malcalester Park Publishing Co.

Saul, Leon J., *Emotional Maturity: The Development and Dynamics of Personality*, J. B. Lippincott Co.

Schindler, John A., *How To Live 365 Days a Year*, Prentice-Hall, Inc.

Shoemaker, Helen Smith, *Power Through Prayer Groups: Their Why and How*, Fleming H. Revell Co.

————, *The Secret of Effective Prayer*, Fleming H. Revell Co.

Shoemaker, Samuel M., *By the Power of God*, Harper & Brothers.

————, *The Experiment of Faith*, Harper & Brothers.

Steiner, Lee R., *Where Do People Take Their Troubles?*, International Universities Press, Inc.

Stolz, Karl R., *The Psychology of Religious Living*, Abingdon Press.

Van Buskirk, James D., *Religion, Healing and Health*, Macmillan Co.

Weatherhead, Leslie D., *Psychology, Religion and Healing*, Abingdon Press.